NIKKEN

EXPERIENCE, INTEGRATED

MICRO
TO MACRO
120 YEARS OF INNOVATION

NIKKEN SEKKEI

MICRO TO MACRO

120 YEARS OF INNOVATION

RIZZOLI
NEW YORK

New York · Paris · London · Milan

Something unaltered
over thousands of years
and something altered
according to a change of era,
have the same origin.
It is the concept between
permanence and temporality.

Matsuo Bashō (1644-1694)

The circularity of life and a distinctly Japanese sense of unfolding time are reflected in the essential philosophy of Nikken Sekkei, the oldest and one of the largest architectural firms in Japan and the world. This idea of an "eternal now", when beginnings and endings are continuous qualities of the same experience, are evident in the company's historical journey as well as in the evolution of the conditions, social needs, and planned responses of Japan over the last 120 years; shaping the country's rebirth and contemporary life.

Legendary Japanese poet Bashõ alludes to this "permanent value" which prepares for and maneuvers the waves of inevitable change. This same spirit of enduring architecture permeates what Nikken Sekkei holds dear and sets it apart from some comparable firms and projects in the world, as it aims for a quintessentially universal aesthetic while at the same time holding onto its founding identity. Japan well knows that change is the only true permanence within the singular forces of nature and society, and that there exists a "poetic spirit" fueling the creative tension in all great works of art and industry. This principle of *fueki ryuko* (不易流行) is timeless and only the ways in which it is expressed vary as time goes on.

Nikken Sekkei has always focused on the power of ingenuity as an expression of beauty, resilience, and contemporaneity, utilizing a self-defined orthodox approach alongside progressive methodologies and strategies. Having navigated more than a century of immense social and economic challenges, it reflects Japan's own persistent drive for self-renewal and maturation in establishing its unique brand of cosmopolitanism. This intuitive power to adapt to society's shifting needs and desires has proven to be of vital importance in the company's collective evolution and innovations over time.

People-focused, sustainable, and value-added design is part of its tangible signature and forms the basis of its prominence and trusted position within Japanese society and in the world. Its reputation for quality environments that strive to positively engage with the natural world is embedded in its DNA; and its age-old traditions of project management, interdisciplinary production, and highly qualified specialists on large but flexible platforms allow for projects that are simply unattainable in many conventional Western atelier style settings.

This anniversary volume is a celebration of the talent, dedication, and resourcefulness of the countless hearts and minds that have accompanied Japan in its current configurations. As a visual survey, it showcases a selection of projects in Nikken Sekkei's extraordinary architectural story and recalls key elements of the company's identity, legacy, and achievements.

Adopting a "micro to macro" perspective, this publication aims to explore design elements – shapes and surfaces – and their manifestations – spaces and environments – within significant structures and settings. Some of these projects are national and international icons, while others are nestled in their respective landscapes. All of them are as much a tribute to the decades of commitment by Nikken Sekkei's employees as to the perpetual development of Japan and global design culture as a whole.

From engineering the movement of millions of people in Tokyo to the quiet elegance of a guest's private window onto a surrounding water body in Kyoto, people everywhere have always referred to the skies to express their aspirations for today, as well as to share their collective visions for the future.

不易流行

1900-1940s

Modernization and the integration of Western ideals

Japan was closed to the rest of the world for more than 250 years during the Tokugawa shogunate (1603-1867), evolving a unique culture which still strongly defines it as the world's third-largest economy. Edo, later renamed as Tokyo, had a vast population in the 1700s and its evolution happened internally rather than by external pressures. Although the Dutch were already trading through Nagasaki, it was not until 1853 upon the arrival of American fleets that the country began fully participating in foreign trade.

Founded in 1900 in Osaka, twenty-six professionals embarked on a brave journey as Japan was rapidly pressing forward with the processes of modernization and the assimilation of Western architectural styles and techniques. This initiative marked the birth of the company with the Sumitomo Head Office Temporary Architecture Department in Osaka.

From the outset, a pioneering approach to technology became one of the fundamental tenets of the fledgling company. Its founders, architects Magoichi Noguchi and Yutaka Hidaka, were an integral part of the cultural, artistic, and innovative fervor of the Japanese cultural elite at the end of the nineteenth century and into the early 1920s. European influences and Victorian styles are clearly evident in their earliest projects. Western life not only opened doors to new aesthetic choices but also to the second industrial revolution and Japan's transformation, which brought a great surge of energy to industries and businesses that understood and applied these innovative techniques and new ways of seeing. Since then the country has continually imported and assimilated elements from other cultures in order to enrich its own. Such purposeful, selective borrowing has been systematically coupled with the ability to translate, refine, and internalize what is newly acquired within well-developed and flexible indigenous Japanese cultural frameworks.

Indeed, Nikken Sekkei's locally focused, environmentally conscious design ethos and commitment was established early on. Its ancestors, the Sumitomo Family in the Meiji Era (1868-1912), gained their fortune from copper as owners of the renowned Besshi Mines in the Ehime Prefecture and a secondary banking business in Japan. The Taisho Era (1912-1926) saw the dynamic development of many domestic and foreign economic objectives, without Japan suffering the colonial fate of other Asian nations, and its enthusiasm for Western culture continued throughout this extraordinarily liberal, yet brief period. However, three devastating events literally shook the country: World War I (1914-18), the Great Kanto Earthquake (1923), and the Great Depression (1929). Fortunately, the solidity and flexibility of Sumitomo's companies withstood these catastrophes and became a winning business strategy. Drastic measures were taken to ensure the company's survival, reducing its employees from 140 to 30 people.

Its leading architects at the time, Eikichi Hasebe and Kenzo Takekoshi, both with experience in the West, willingly left to establish an architectural design office for their loyal staff, supported by the Sumitomo Partnership Firm. This bold initiative afforded a historic opportunity to realize the iconic Osaka Stock Exchange building. The firm also gained the commission for the Tokyo Commercial Paper Clearing House and subsequently the headquarters for the Nippon Life Insurance Company, as well as many other fundamental projects. A decade later their staff grew to 250 members.

One of the best examples of their legendary legacy in this early part of the 20th century is the **Osaka Prefectural Nakanoshima Library (1904)**, a stately building in neo-Baroque style with three-layered stone walls and a rising sheet-copper roofed dome, designed by Noguchi and Hidaka. It is one of the oldest, western architectural style libraries in Japan and a nationally important cultural property.

Work on the company's long-awaited headquarters culminated with its preeminent **Sumitomo Building (1930)** in Osaka, which aimed to foster transparency and trust with a monumental combination of purpose and symbolism that is silently protected by a disaster prevention design. This large, rectangular stone building surrounds a single-story skylit banking hall, safeguarding a richly articulated and decorative interior, and remains a canonical work in the history of both the Hasebe-Takekoshi office and the subsequent development of the Nikken Sekkei firm.

Economic considerations were clearly paramount during the 1930s and these buildings were generally more functionally oriented than their predecessors, owing to the growing need for anti-seismic still-frames and reinforced-concrete constructions, alongside the pro-Rationalist mindset which Japan and other industrialized nations shared at the time.

Expressions of monumental yet stripped neoclassicism that could be modernized or rendered more explicitly representational with the use of columns and pediments defined a confident architectural style for the new capitalist economy. The **Osaka Securities Exchange Building (1935)** began serving as a tangible manifestation of this kind of implicit authority. Featuring a grand, white cylindrical facade and lobby with superb stained-glass ornamentation, its social significance dates back to the Edo period. And its generous, weighty, and modern air-conditioned offices, trading floor, and oval-shaped entrance still accommodate some 2,000 people.

A few years later, the **Nippon Life Insurance Company Head Office (1939)** in Osaka was the first to showcase an elegantly understated granite exterior defying the hardships of its turbulent history. Its construction was begun by the Hasebe-Takekoshi Architects' Office but while facing many obstacles - from the Second Sino-Japanese War to the onslaught of World War II, when the building was confiscated by Allied Occupation Forces - it was finally completed in 1962 and still stands as a bastion of security.

1950-1990s

Towards security, efficiency, and prosperity

In the decade after World War II, Japan experienced a tumultuous time that roughly divided the history of Nikken Sekkei. The country's devastation presented a pivotal turning point for every aspect of life, as people were forced to literally face "ground zero". With the courage and relentless spirit of this generation to begin again, the company was able to reincarnate from its technological experience and profound beliefs in a better future. Industrial infrastructures had suffered great damage and the ensuing Allied Occupation, from 1945 to 1952, also led to the imposed dismantling of Japan's largest enterprises. Sumitomo ingeniously established a general trading company absorbing repatriated Japanese workers from overseas and this business lifeline gave rise to the Nippon Engineering Co. Ltd., which served as a practical omen for the country's rebirth.

The early 1950s was a time of intense learning and consolidation, and one of the company's greatest priorities was to catapult itself across the technological chasm created by the war. Architecture, like other art forms and cultural life in Japan, began to experience a sense of abiding freedom. A youthful energy determined to rebuild its cities as "ideal states" eluded any strict adherence to conventions or aesthetic limitations. Post-war modernism - fed by the booming metallurgic economy during the war in Korea - gave Japan the unprecedented opportunity to cultivate a vibrant liberal economy and a new democracy, which brought rapid urbanization, lifestyle changes, inherent trust in advanced technologies, and the pervasive eagerness to reconstruct society, based on renewed principles of excellence and endurance.

The commercial boom of the late 1950s and '60s marked the zenith in Japan's "economic miracle", with phenomenal progress in the country's industrialization and technological capacities, lasting well into the 1970s and '80s. During those prodigious years Japan went far beyond repairing its wartime wounds to becoming an industrial superpower.

The succession of companies since its early days as the Sumitomo Temporary Architecture Department evolved a consistency of shared values, integrated skills and collaborative vision, which have been passed on like a cultural baton across generations of employees at Nikken Sekkei.

In 1962 a new management system was introduced, with high-level, combined engineering competencies in tertiary industry construction, based on trusted partners, accomplished designers, and resilient project manager relationships. In 1970 the company changed its name to its current iteration as Nikken Sekkei Ltd., with the English version borrowing the tagline: "planners, architects, engineers".

In 1972 the issue of limited resources reappeared and the question of how to exploit the country's natural reserves while ensuring its environmental safety led to the company's development of an array of award-winning energy saving plans, strategies and technologies. Since then, sustainability has been a central concern for all its projects. And despite the 1970s world oil crisis, the Japanese economy entered a period of stable growth, followed by an impressive export expansion in the 1980s which confirmed its international competitiveness.
As its cities grew larger and more complex, new urban contexts presented architectural challenges, requiring high-tech solutions. Large-scale mixed-use projects materialized, and spacious atriums filled with natural light, offering panoramic views of the world outside, became increasingly popular. Movement, efficiency and stylish simplicity became paramount in both the designers' and end-users' imaginations. Within the financial fervor, working hours were extended and people's offices doubled as their protracted living spaces.

Designing for high-rise buildings, engineering for resourceful exteriors and planning increasingly sophisticated information technologies were meticulously researched and developed. This growing demand for quality workspaces in urban environments consolidated Nikken Sekkei's reputation and led to numerous major projects throughout the 1990s.

With its prototypical works, not only at the macro level of mega-structures but also at the micro interstitial level, such as responsive exterior membranes and special flooring systems, the company continued to work proactively and progressively toward the physical and environmental challenges of both climate and urbanization.

Still guarding the heart of Ginza, the **San-ai Dream Center (1963)** is one of their most recognizable landmarks in Tokyo. Among the first buildings in Japan to utilize light as an influential urban element - balancing the aesthetics of tradition and modernity - its transparent glass cylinder perimeter and ceiling are almost entirely filled with lighting fixtures. At night the building is an enticingly illuminated showcase on the capital's most famous shopping strip and continues to reflect the city's contemporary energy.

Another iconic project of the same period, intended as an archetype for the future of Tokyo and a modern Japan, is the **Palaceside Building (1966)**. First in a series of long-span office buildings inaugurating the development of truly multi-purpose architecture, it totaled 119,700 square meters upon completion and is still one of the largest masterworks in Japan. Its exceptionally striking cylindrical towers and articulated elevations form a system of delicately detailed metallic louvers and vertical rain spouts with extensive glass surfaces that provide solar protection, as well as plasticity and assertive rhythm throughout its enormous volume. After a long economic boom, the Japanese economy was jolted by a sharp plunge in its real estate market of the 1990s, when the country experienced serious setbacks. In response to this, Nikken Sekkei began investing in the realization of environmental architectures around the world, thereby establishing its global presence.

The **Islamic Development Bank Headquarters (1993)** located in Jeddah, Saudi Arabia, manifests this winning creativity on a grand scale. Detailed topographical studies were carried out to harmonize the building with its local climate and integrate its distinctive Islamic design with modern architectural systems. Its linear majesty invokes its irrefutable positioning close to the Red Sea, with unique energy conservation strategies, such as narrow slit-like fenestrations and an octagonal roof, creating an elegant central light-court with spectacularly tessellated skylights.

From the same period, a pioneering example of the synergy between mixed-used development and transit-oriented development is **Queen's Square Yokohama (1997)** in Japan's Kanagawa Prefecture, which clearly resonates with its urban setting and sustainability objectives. Intended as a model of future urbanism and one of the centerpieces of the Minato Mirai district, directly connected to the station, it consists of three large-scale office blocks, Yokohama Bay Hotel Tokyu, the Minato Mirai Hall, the Queen Mall, and the Minatomirai Tokyu Square. Notably this integrated block plan, networking both indoor and outdoor pedestrian promenades, forms a continuous skyline of stepped and undulating edges with three towers decreasing in height as they approach the sea; commanding a spectacular view of this famed port opening onto Tokyo Bay.

2000s-present
Development and sustainability in a global culture

Nikken Sekkei's greatest strength surely lies in its comprehensive organizational networks and capabilities, which integrate the expertise of talented designers, urban planners, architects, engineers, construction managers, and researchers. With its allied group companies, it has stretched its vision from the minute detailing of interiors to the complexity of streetscapes, and through to the transformation of entire districts. Without acquisitions or mergers, it has not only retained its prominence over the last century but is evermore synonymous with expert confidence, realizing over 25,000 projects across more than 250 cities and 50 countries. From its extraordinary local beginnings, the company has established itself in China, South Korea, Vietnam, Singapore, India, Thailand, the UAE, Russia, and Europe, and is currently evolving dedicated centers of excellence in highly specialized sectors.

Our digital age manifests epochal shifts from the conventional industries established by the Industrial Revolution into nascent economies that are increasingly based on information and robotics. Transitioning into this highly technological existence and experimenting with striking new forms, surfaces, and climatic solutions, Nikken Sekkei is once again a pioneer in the integration and application of engineering data in transformative ways.

At the turn of this century, the company demonstrates strong commitment to building across Asia, where urban development has been particularly dynamic over the last two decades. The world is now tackling the need to achieve low carbon driven societies, an effective and longer-term equilibrium with nature, as well as societal stability and security. Correspondingly, the many challenges for architecture and urban planning call for increasingly higher-order responses. This kind of inventiveness and adaptation are epitomized in Nikken Sekkei's many spectacularly flexible and solution-driven creations, such as the **Saitama Super Arena (2000)** in Japan which expands and contracts with a smaller arena within one of the largest stadiums in the world; and the **Japanese Red Cross Ishinomaki Hospital (2011)** in Miyagi Prefecture, a model par excellence in disaster preparedness, which serves as a community center with sophisticated security strategies and a renowned "escape map" that is used across Japan and in other countries.

An international landmark, the **Tokyo Skytree (2012)** is currently the world's tallest free-standing broadcasting tower, serving as the primary television and radio site for the Kantō region. The Skytree's pioneering structural design, applying *shimbashira seishin* (central column vibration control), features cutting-edge engineering technologies enabling it to withstand tremors and winds by utilizing an independent outer frame of steel piping and pre-stressed concrete. The name was derived from traditional Japanese architectures like the five-story pagoda and this system effectively absorbs seismic activity and functions as the centerpiece of a large commercial development. This magnificent "mechanical tree" stands as a giant in a virtual forest of skyscrapers, paying homage to its valiant predecessor, the **Tokyo Tower (1958)**, also designed by Nikken Sekkei to accommodate the beginning of television in the country and remains a period monument to Japan's rising economic strength. Based on the priorities of safety and elegance, both these structures personify a signature of efficiency and precision.

The company's initiatives in China have also been much applauded, such as its construction of the **Shanghai Greenland Center (2017)** which has established an "urban farm" in the middle of the city. As a major transport hub located above a two-line subway station, this ambitious project features interconnected, semi-outdoor avenues that allow for the free circulation of thousands of visitors, bringing lush vegetation to a built-up area.

This versatile concept of a self-sustaining and socially engaging "urban core" is also beautifully demonstrated in the once-in-a-century mega-project underway in Tokyo's central station zone. With the completion of its first eastern tower, **Shibuya Scramble Square (2019)** forms impressive connections between the city's transport services, its social dynamism, and the country's cultural transmission to the rest of the world. Breaking away from the usual partitioning of super high-rise buildings, this refreshing design emerges from an exclusively lithe base that responds to the flow of people. Vertical apertures, doubling as natural ventilation systems, interpose its enormous glass facade and openly embrace the vitality of the streets. The entire structure pulsates with Shibuya's distinctive vigor, overlooking Mt. Fuji silhouetted against Tokyo's glittering night skies.

Many projects in the Middle East also highlight the company's design transferability. Most recently, the **One Za'abeel (2022)** in Dubai is already a symbol of elegance within an extremely competitive skyline. Consisting of a high-rise, mixed-use luxury development, it forms a panoramic aerial concourse connecting two towers and creates the gateway of the old and new Dubai. Its construction has reached a new milestone with the launch of the sliding phase of the world's largest cantilevered structure. Suspended 100 meters above ground and measuring 210 meters in length, this timeless configuration already serves as a truly immersive experience.

Community facilities with multi-level specialization, particularly in transport initiatives, are evident in groundbreaking works such as Singapore's extraordinary **Rail Corridor (2011)** landscape project, connecting 24 kilometers of continuous community space that spans the entire nation. The company has also master-planned Russia's first major transport and housing development (2014) around northern Moscow's Botanichesky Sad Station, revitalizing the banks of the Yauza river. In Europe, its **Futur Camp Nou (2025)** project is underway, which is an ambitious remodeling of the revered FC Barcelona stadium, expressing the club's famed egalitarian identity with three 360-degree concourses and open terraces running along its entire perimeter. This highly original plan aims to transform the conventional exterior facade so that spectators standing on each concourse can feel part of its surrounding cityscape.

As Nikken Sekkei has shown throughout its remarkable longevity, many of the best reflections from the past can flashback and inspire our contemporary creativity; much like one's own treasured memories enrich and develop everyday experience. This "everlasting now", represented in both art and architecture, forms the palimpsest of shapes, surfaces, spaces, and environments to which we can all relate.

CONTENTS

S H A P E S

Geometric proportions are an enduring foundation of human culture and design; from the elaborate ornamentation found in ageless architectures, to the complex fractals of contemporary artworks, or the smooth sculpturing of ultra-modern interiors. We see patterning everywhere in flora and fauna - from unicellular formations through to stellar systems - and tessellations of such universal morphologies engage us both intellectually and emotionally.

Designing relationships between people, buildings and environments, biophilic planning makes use of the "rationality" in nature's diversity.

Pervasive in Japanese architecture and the visual arts is an appreciation for the natural world as a tangible source of spiritual and creative insights. Indigenous sensibilities, long-preceding Buddhism, saw this transcendent realm - exemplified in nature's architectures such as shells, trees, and mountains - regulating all living beings through the perpetual cycles of birth, fruition, and decay.

Nikken Sekkei's characteristically pristine minimalism magnifies these vital shapes into meaningful structures that correlate with people and their settings.

Its **Kakegawa City Hall (1996)** in Japan's Shizuoka Prefecture, which replaces the original municipal building also designed by the company, is one such topographical centerpiece surrounded by parkland. Pioneering environmentally conscious design, it takes full advantage of the natural light and ventilation, as well as the recycling of water, with an impressive cockle shell style atrium over a predominantly rectangular building. This majestic double-conical volume is easily recognizable from afar and finished in polished aluminum with seam lines forming beautiful radial patterns.

The building's entrance is bordered by large transparent glass surfaces, interplaying with light and shadow, which create an unexpected sense of lightness throughout and enhance the combination of two bold shapes, suggesting stability and harmony.

Kakegawa City Hall

Quintessential forms, built to last and to adapt both conceptually and functionally, are strong features in the company's realizations over the last century. Circular motifs lending timelessness and harmony, as well as open plan interiors, interconnecting floors and planes with multifaceted light wells, have incorporated both visual complexity and order into the fabric of their spaces, and potentially in the behavioral culture of those inhabiting them. Such is the case with the metaphorical "enlightenment" offered by the splendid blue corbeled dome of the main students' hall at **Tsurumi University (1997)** in Yokohama, with its concentric layers leading to the sky; or the massive rotunda of the logistics terminal in Tokyo's **Yamato Group Haneda Chronogate (2013)**, which practically revolutionized the organizational model of an industrial complex by including community services, like open forums and childcare facilities.

This clever continuum of curved spaces and rounded features, connecting internal and external environments, provides for enhanced architectural adaptability and more organically inspired relationships with the public.

Osaka Prefectural Nakanoshima Library

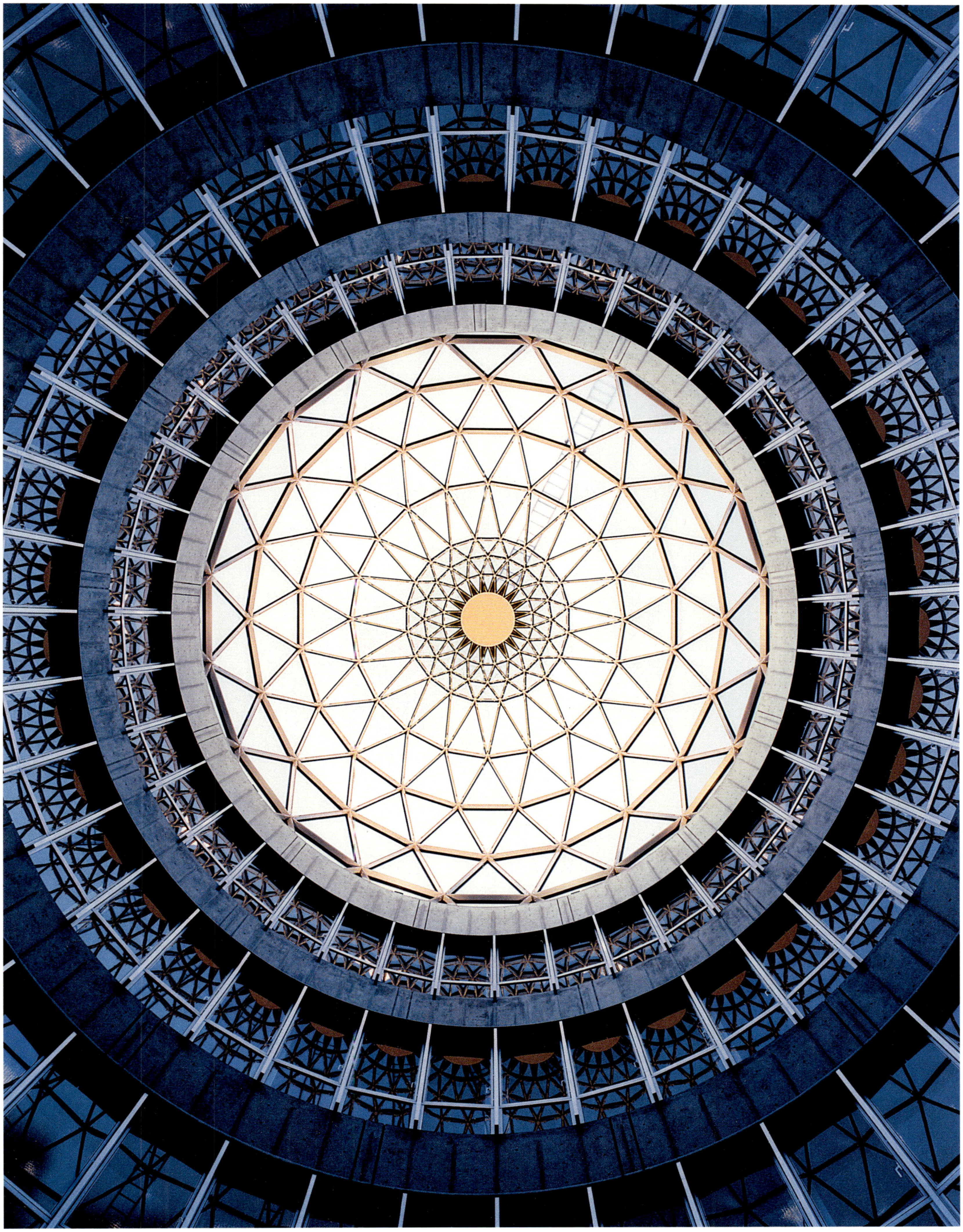

Tsurumi University

Palaceside Building

Mitsui Sumitomo Insurance Surugadai Building and Surugadai Annex Building

Kobe International House

Toslove Hakone Viole

Japan Pavilion Expo 70

According to Zen principles, the *ensō* (円相) or "circular form" symbolizes absolute clarity and perfection in the swiftly expressive brushstroke of a calligrapher's hand.

This ancient notion of a creatively charged void, emerging from Japanese minimalist aesthetics, offers a conceptual framework to enliven and unite a passageway between two otherwise separate dimensions in the case of the **Osaka City Air Terminal (1996)**, with its underground moving walkway facilitating the largest bus terminal in western Japan.

This remarkable forerunner of lighting and space management changes appearance as it interacts with thousands of pedestrians along its sinuous glass walls and softly illuminated ceiling shapes. Patterns of contrasting colors and shadows alternate throughout a surprisingly incandescent urban corridor that efficiently connects the country from north to south.

Both the logistical challenges and the psychological sensations of continuous human movement through time and space are complemented by this inspired design. Balanced by the addition of a full-scale rooftop garden, the entire structure offers an inner-city oasis linking its subterranean experience with the outside world.

Osaka City Air Terminal (OCAT)

Enlightenment, strength, elegance, the universe and the void; the circle is perfection encompassing all other shapes.

San-Ai Dream Center

San-Ai Dream Center

ASTRA HELIPORT
ASTRA HELIPORT

Overseeing the heart of Jakarta, the **Menara Astra (2017)** building is a landmark for the city and serves as the headquarters of one of Indonesia's largest conglomerates.

Its double-sided glass frontage design embraces the entire tower in a clasped-hands formation, materializing its corporate philosophy of cultural connectedness and international cooperation.

Symbolic connotations of unity and commitment on such a grand scale are achieved by a distinctively oblong tubular cladding, rising fifty floors above its urban environment, like the interlocking spurs found in natural landscapes. Its unique shape directs the prevailing winds away from the building and wards off turbulence to provide stability and protection.

Menara Astra

Mode Gakuen Spiral Towers

Osaka World Trade Center Building (Cosmo Tower)

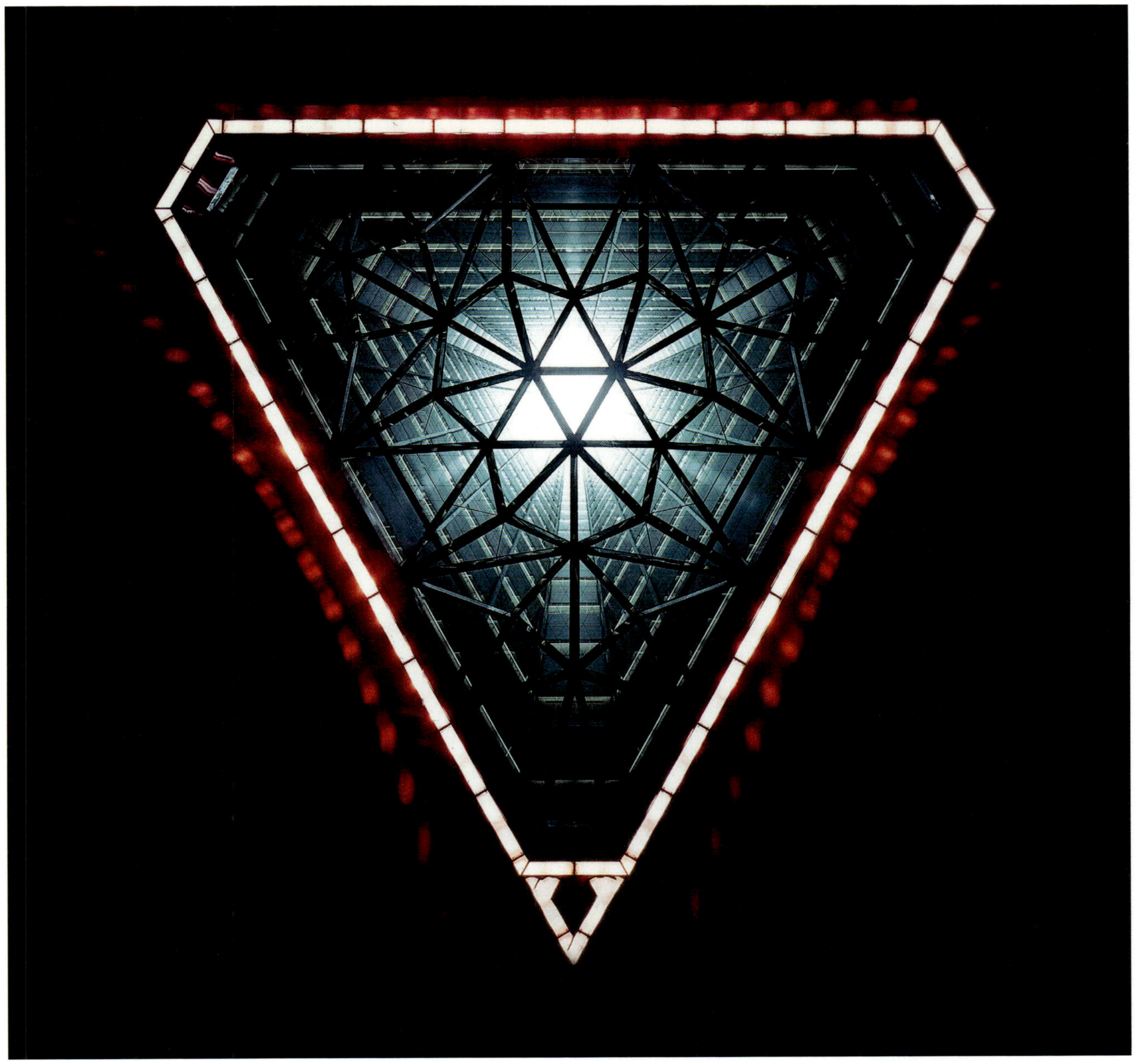

Shinjuku Sumitomo Building

Triangular motifs are innately dynamic, especially with increasingly sophisticated contemporary architectures. Viewed from various angles, they evoke both direction and exploration. Sometimes provocative or assertive, at other times more stoic and dignified, these shapes achieve myriad visual possibilities and powerful structural tapestries.

Such kaleidoscopic patterns are celebrated in the **Shinjuku Sumitomo Building (1974)** in Tokyo, which Nikken Sekkei also renovated in 2020 with new spaces that re-elaborate its original elements and ambiance. Affectionately called the *Sankaku* (triangle) for its striking interior and exterior touches, this earlier design presents a massive pyramidal glass atrium that runs through the entire height of the building, filling it with light. The same concept has now been extended to create a new plaza at its base.

This merging of interior and exterior spaces is also showcased in the triangular confidence of the **Osaka World Trade Center Building (1995)**. Its deltoid formation emboldens the glass-walled elevator shafts and creates an interesting prism effect. Aptly referred to as the "Cosmo Tower", it pioneered high-rise buildings in the country.

From intricate, interwoven facade-forming spirals, such as in the **Mode Gakuen Spiral Towers (2008)** in Nagoya, Japan, to slanted masses and protruding angular forms, ubiquitous triangles often take engineering and construction feats to the next level, such as the **Guangzhou Library (2012)** in China. Housing some 3.5 million books, this building is the world's largest open-stack public library.

Conceived as a Chinese logogram, its exterior simulates piles of books with randomly distributed stone louvers jutting from its deep-set windows. Softer, sculptural shapes inside, like its transparent elevators and escalators, create a sense of visual unity that welcomes readers of all ages and asserts the building's mission as a physically unfolding "treasure trove" of knowledge.

Literally and metaphorically, rectangular and squared shapes are strong foundational building blocks that support elements like bricks, beams, and columns. Our familiarity with these shapes facilitates a sense of reliability, while their perfect angles lend authority and formality to such architectures.

Nikken Sekkei's long-standing plans with the Japan Radio Company culminated in the distinctive **JRC Advanced Technology Center (2014)**, located in Nagano. Resembling a huge stack of rectangular slabs, this cleverly playful design affords ingeniously expanding workspaces dedicated to experimentation, with various layers of integrated space.

Overhanging balconies in all directions and a spiral-like open ceiling in the center connect every floor, like a chimney effect. Spearheading both companies' environmental imperatives for natural lighting, ventilation, and solar power, this innovative design suggests both stability and creativity.

JRC

Midland Square

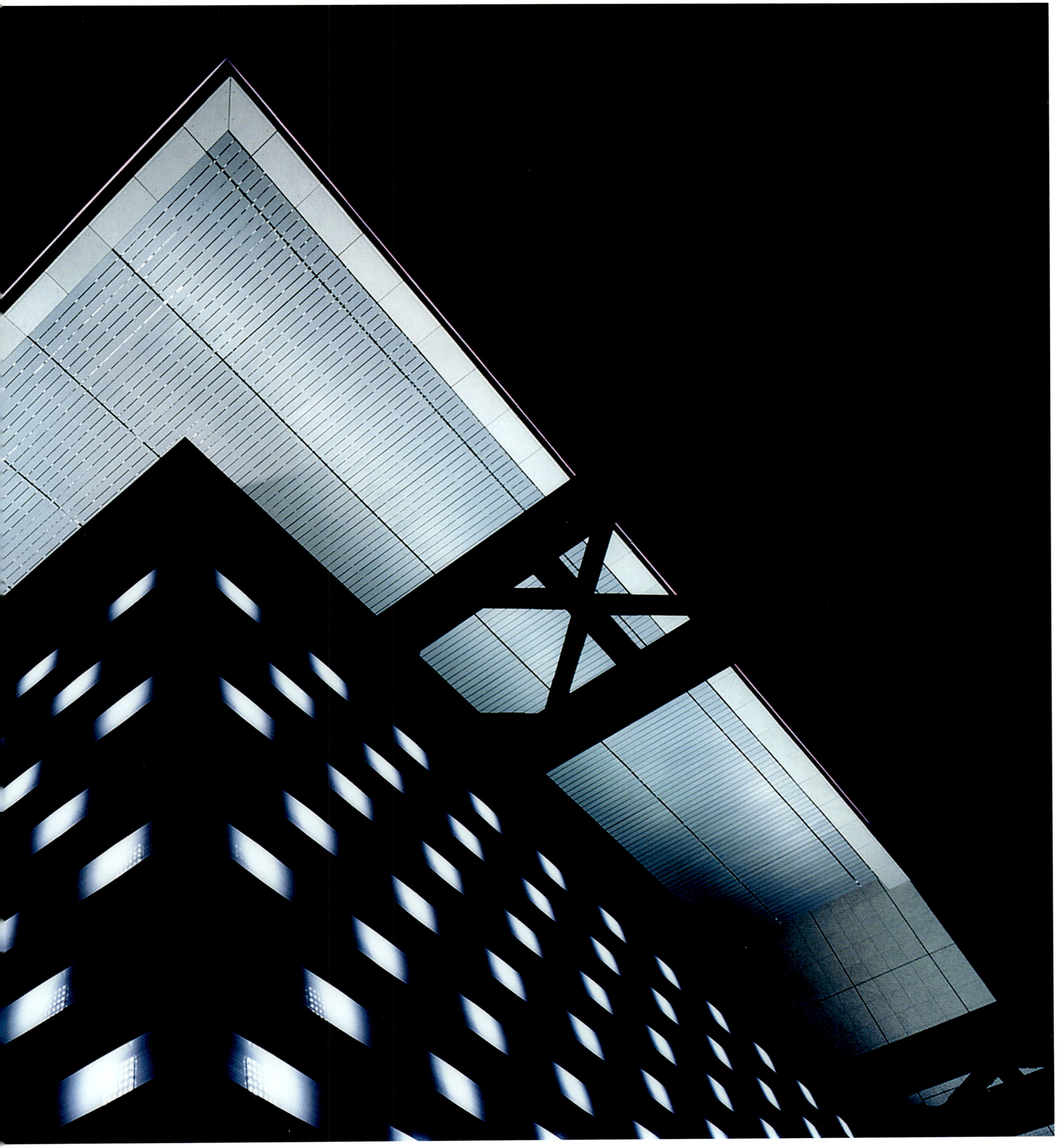

Symmetrical repetition is like a chant; it has the power to hypnotize, like visual meditation.

St Luke's International Hospital

A massive rectangular hollow is the key feature of the **NEC Head Office (1990)**, popularly known in Tokyo as the "Super-Tower".

Nikken Sekkei's aerodynamic solution for this building applies a tunnel concept running through its entire center, diffusing the wind energy and illuminating the atrium.

A prevailing skyscraper in this high-density area, it conveys a certain gravitas and dependability, in line with the cultural identity of an information and electronics giant.

More inviting than some conventional high-rise structures of its time, it is well protected on the street level by sheer perpendicular surfaces, providing a unique "urban window" for various interactions with the community.

NEC Head Office (NEC Super Tower)

Squares also connote a kind of earthly and material excellence that is constant and reassuring. Softened by internal circular formations, together they can even represent a connection between the human and divine realms.

One of Nikken Sekkei's award-winning cultural buildings which quite literally defies gravity is the **Hoki Museum (2010)** in Chiba's largest park. As Japan's first private art museum dedicated to Realist paintings, its rectangular box-shaped design translates to a spectacularly seamless ensemble of lithe and overlapping tubular spaces that are reminiscent of a biological exoskeleton. Melding confidently with its verdant setting, it could be considered a contemporary artwork in its own right.

Instead of the commonplace and homogenous "white cube" concept, with blandly square walls and ceiling lights, this supple and open yet guided architectural idea encourages curiosity and exploration along its 500-meter viewing route, segmented into individual galleries on three floors that connect to a wide cantilevered head at the entrance. This building's exceptional "site-specific" cuboid design has effectively re-staged the conventional art space and its relationship with the works on display.

Like a kind of Rubik's Cube offering limitless possibilities and chance happenings, the **Toho Gakuen School of Music (2014)** in Tokyo was intended to facilitate creativity and openness within its unfolding spaces.

Constructing a feeling of continuity and smooth accessibility, the main body of this building is kept to the first and second basement floors, freeing up the ground level as a campus. On its upper and lower floors, a porous, connective box-like volume with unevenly spaced columns inspires impromptu meetings and performances in a conservatoire environment.

This design was a novel attempt to break away from the typically confined spaces of college settings and to satisfy the need for completely soundproof rehearsal rooms, as well as to provide for visual stimuli and personalized connections among the musicians.

Okata Port Passenger Shelter / Tsunami Evacuation Facility

Curves and spirals
are tangible feats;
capturing infinity and
giving us the freedom
to imagine what
our eyes cannot see.

Marukyu Building

Spirals in architecture can represent the notion of evolution and mystery, taking people on a journey that inspires fantasy and wonder.

Featured in the entrance of Japan's **Conrad Osaka (2017)** luxury hotel, atop the Nakanoshima Festival Tower West which overlooks the Dojima and Tosabori rivers, there is a remarkably beautiful staircase resembling an elegant satin ribbon unraveling for its privileged audience. Leading to the 40th floor of this tower and a double height wall of curved windows framing the city, this splendid interior design recreates an operatic ambiance with its balcony perspectives.

Showcasing the art of Japanese hospitality, with combined touches of antiquity and contemporary art, these sleek white stairs add a celebratory mood to this renowned urban sanctuary in the sky.

Conrad Osaka

Nakanoshima Festival Tower

Nikkei Head Office

Mainichi Broadcasting Headquarters Building

SURFACES

Precise craftsmanship using natural and manufactured materials, multi-functional textures, and state-of-the-art technologies have continued to distinguish Nikken Sekkei as an industry leader.

The intimate beauty and colors of wood or glass are fluently reconciled with the strength and versatility of steel or concrete; enhancing both design and climate-adaptive construction. With each line drawing, its designers seem to invoke their architectural legacy, in quiet devotion to what has come before them. Perhaps this is the essence of the company's sustained innovation across the radically different backdrops of Japan's aesthetic and social histories.

And yet increasingly resilient and interactive buildings with high performance surfaces, destined to become new "cultural properties", clearly require very progressive engineering and planning capabilities for such complex metropolises.

Futuristic flair in the iconic **Sumitomo Fudosan Azabu-Juban Building (2017)** sets the stage for Tokyo's famed dynamism. The variegated, triangular geometries on its shimmering metallic frontage respond to the changing light, almost like a gigantic holographic display. Its slanted aluminum ceiling also reflects and deflects light from streetlights, passing cars and even up-lit trees, conjuring the feeling of time passing. The building's uniquely randomized balconies project onto the spandrel spaces between its floors to highlight this protagonistic design.

An interesting camouflage effect is also achieved by the fish-scale glass facade of the **China International Trust and Investment Corporation (CITIC) Plaza (2010)** in the old city district of Shanghai, using intermittent color across the building's horizontal surfaces. This subtly animated exterior offers a reinterpretation of the city's traditional *lilong* neighborhood lanes and establishes a vital interface with Shanghai's streetscape.

Gracefully concave, a tapestried steel and glass canopy straddles the two spectacular L-shaped matching towers of the **Suzhou Modern Media Plaza (2016)** in China. Positioned like commas punctuating the flow of people, they form a "fifth generation" landmark, symbolizing the motifs from Suzhou's ancient silk trade heritage.

Tokyo's majestic **Shinjuku NS Building (1982)** combines a traditional Japanese "void center" with a typically Western style atrium. Pioneering the latest seismic engineering methods at the time, its flexible corner joints and textured tile cladding formed one of the first mega-projects of the period to explore architectural design possibilities with sunlight. Under its trailblazing sky-bridge it still shelters the world's largest sculptural timepiece.

Sumitomo Fudosan Azabu-Juban Building

CITIC Plaza

Suzhou Modern Media Plaza

Shinjuku NS Building

Okabe Headquarters Building

The impact of a facade is not just aesthetic, it is also the tactile experience you have within the ensemble.

Saitama Super Arena

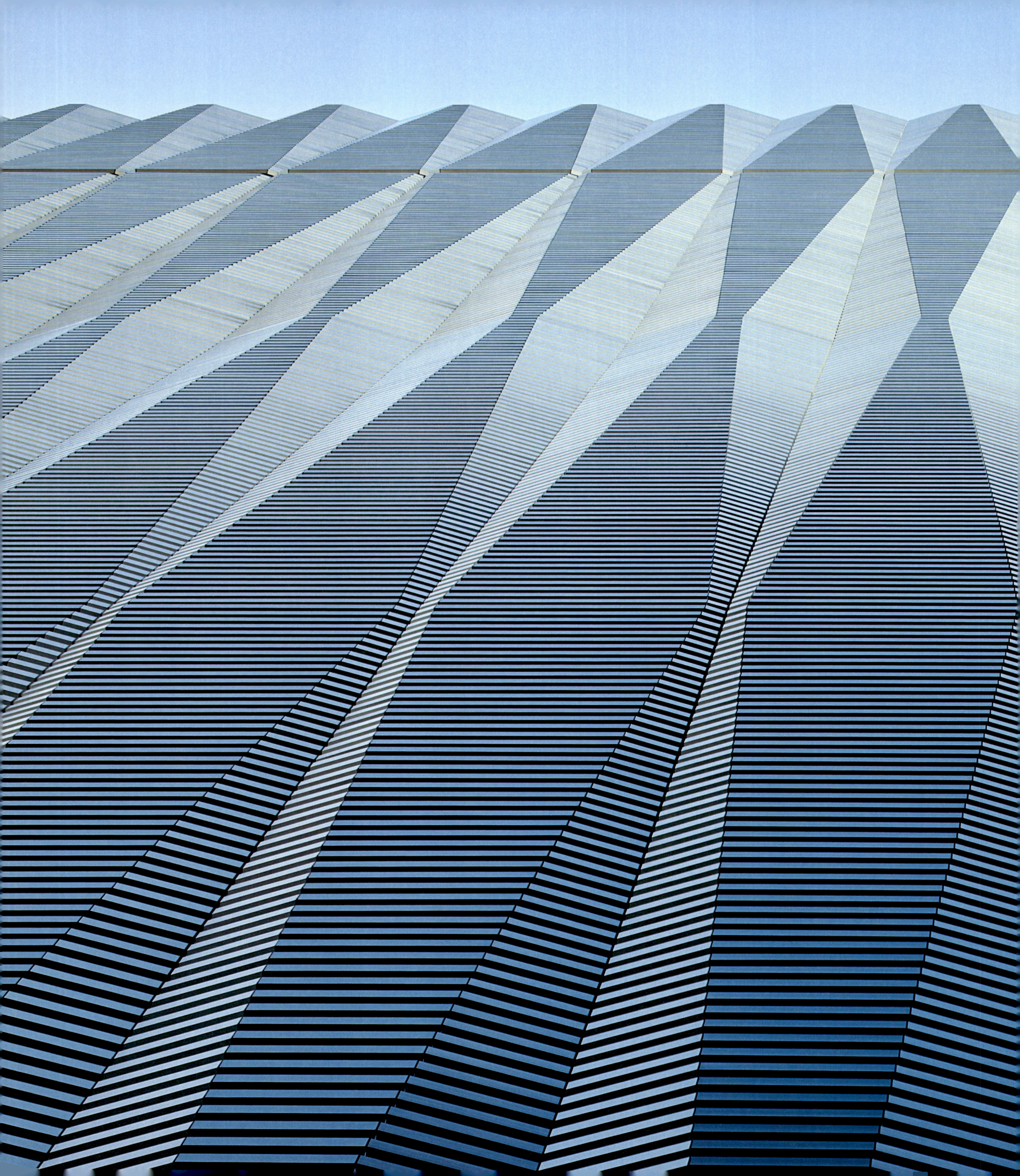

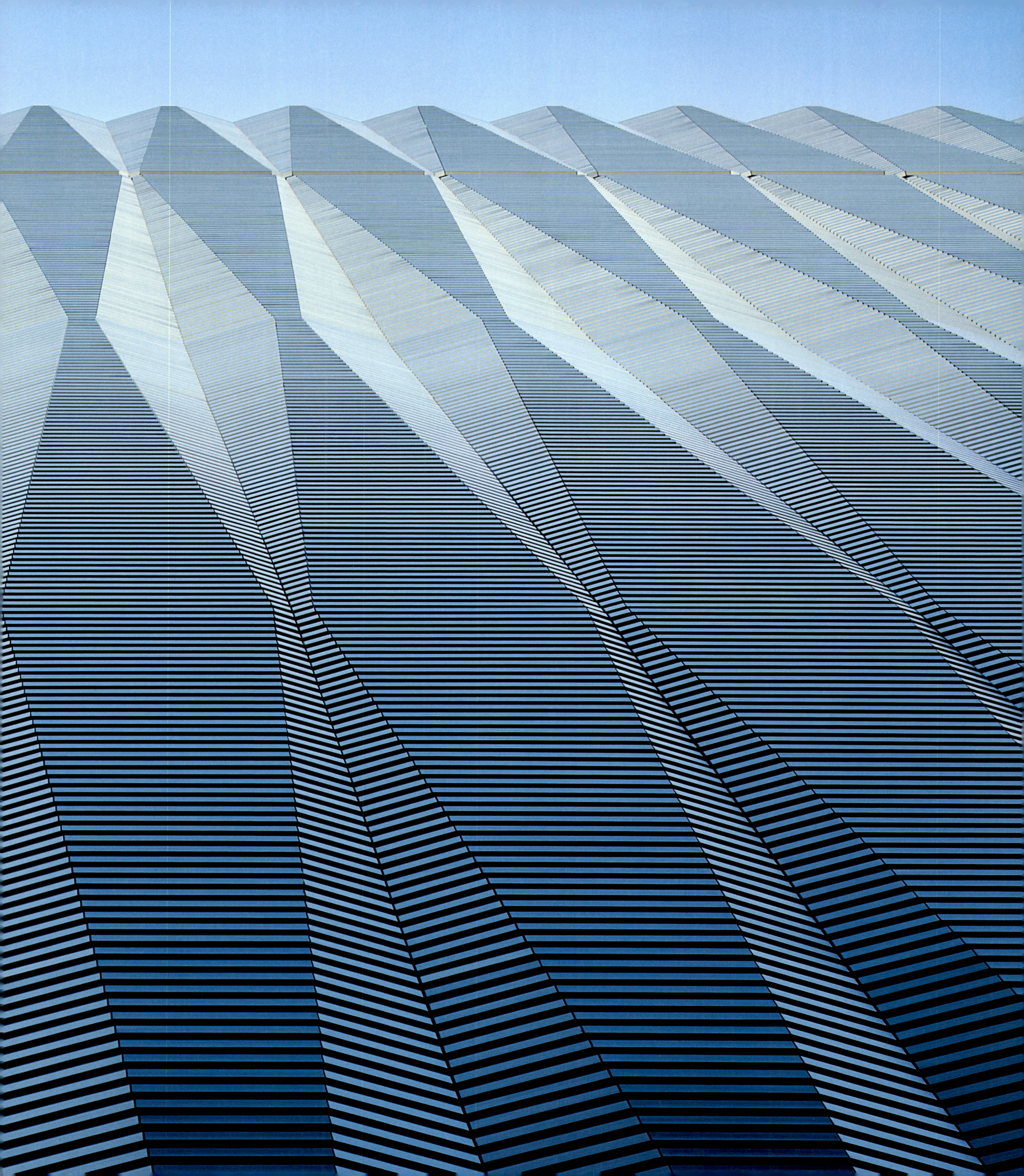

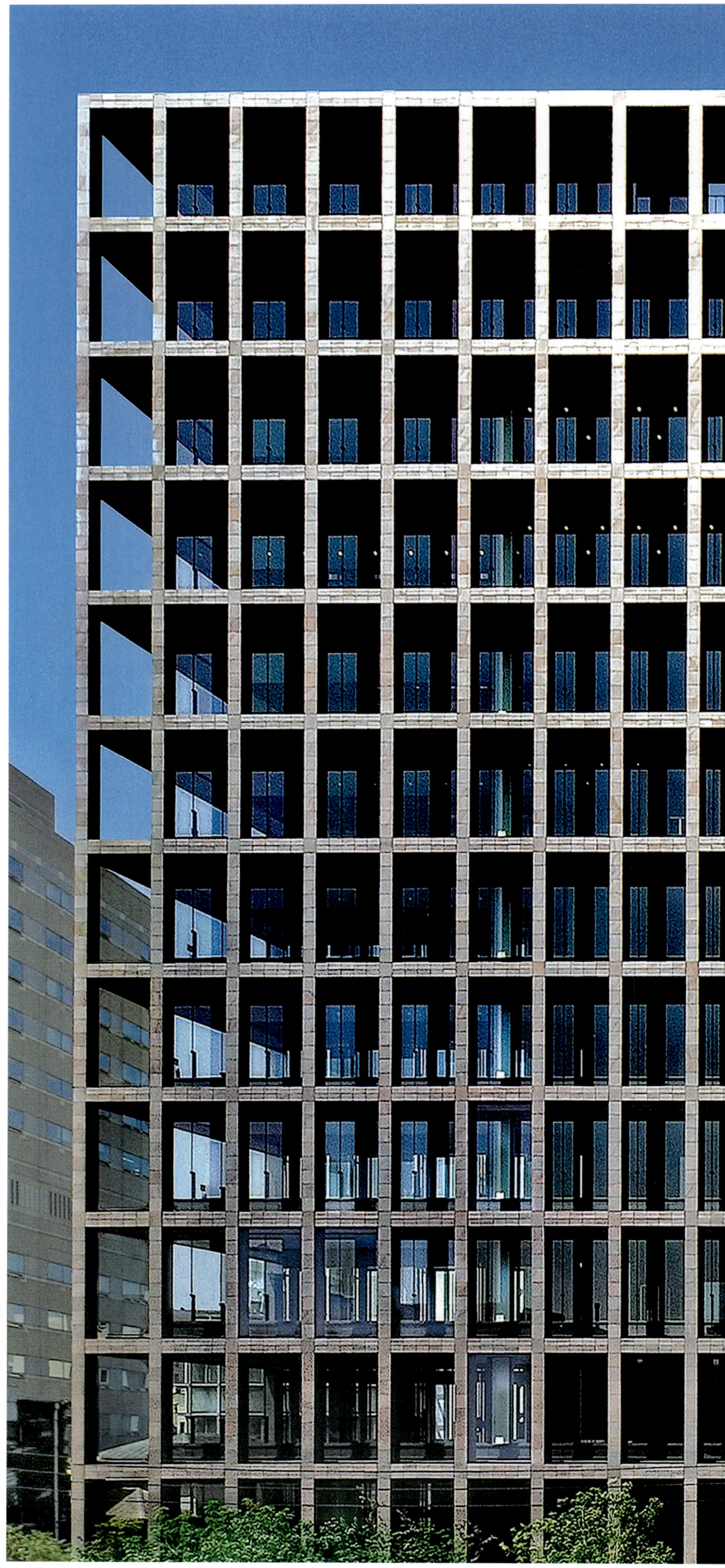

Previous Pages:
Tokyu Plaza Ginza

Osaka Bar Association Building

Mesmerizing optical effects are created by the glazed, rib facade of the **Tokyu Plaza Ginza (2016)**, as the sunshine bounces off its hexagonal pyramid surfaces much like in the morphology of crystals. Inspired by a traditional Edo *kiriko* styled glass motif, supported by an aluminum louvered structure, the building's sculpted exterior was designed to mirror the vitality within the plaza as well as the surrounding streets. An enormous open-air atrium with a multitude of scenic elements creates an exceptional interpretation of urban living possibilities.

The **Osaka Bar Association Building (2006)** overlooks the rivers and parks of this renowned "water city" and embodies the motto of "accessibility to citizens" of this historic institution that dates back to 1880. This elegant, rectangular grid frontage provides for natural light-filled spaces and open external corridors which cultivate an ambience of stability and unrestricted sanctuary.

Exterior pillars and woven lattice beams form a massive sheltered glass box-like structure, adorned with ceramic tiles and brick masonry, adding a feeling of timelessness to its passageways.

A horizontally textured concrete surface coupled with monumental rectangular columns lend authority to the external walls of the **Daiichi Sankyo Shinagawa R & D Center (2016)**, as it connects Japan to the rest of the world; while the checkered contrast of its vertical trapezoid walls and ceiling patterns with a horizontal seating arrangement in the new auditorium of the historic **Waseda University Senior High School (2014)** endows sophisticated elegance to this low-rise building.

Yokohama Mitsui Building

Previous Pages:
Daiichi Sankyo Shinagawa R&D Center

Waseda University Senior High School, Auditorium

Guangzhou Library

Daido Life Insurance Company Osaka Head Office Building

NBF Osaki Building

Wood is embedded
in our soul and traditions;
so familiar, yet contemporary
and alluring in its diverse
architectural possibilities.

Toho Gakuen School of Music

Aichi University of the Arts, Music Department Building

Wood is omnipresent in traditional Japanese architecture. Its natural splendor and ability to yield to its climatic conditions - promoting ventilation and durability - make it a valued choice that adds meaning and materiality to many contemporary buildings. Whether shaping and interlocking large structural elements or embellishing small interior details, the cultural and environmental sovereignty of timber commands our attention, especially in fast-paced inner-city contexts.

The sensual and intricate joineries inside the pioneering **Mokuzai Kaikan (2009)** building revive this potential of wood to reinvigorate urban spaces and afford instinctive appeal. Serving as the office spaces for Tokyo's Lumber Wholesalers Association, every detailed aspect of this beautiful building features the leitmotif of wood.

The **Anan City Office (2017)** in Japan's Tokushima Prefecture also makes generous use of local timber trimmings and furniture to showcase its comforting and uplifting assembly hall.

Anan City Office

Tokyo's **NBF Osaki Building (2011)** displays engineering excellence with its world-first "bioskin" system. As a 25-story research and development complex, it is encircled by deep set balconies with louvered railings made of water-permeable ceramic piping surfaces.

Utilizing accumulated rainwater, this pioneering concept - based on the Japanese summertime tradition of *uchimizu* which refers to the sprinkling of water in gardens and streets - cools down the building's surface area and surrounding air through evaporation while preventing intense sunlight from penetrating its interior.

Applying Nikken Sekkei's time-honored principles of aesthetics working in unison with lasting functionality, this highly innovative frontage contributes to a stimulating yet relaxing visual environment. The practice of bio-inspiration is centuries-old but has only relatively recently progressed to such adaptive technological systems.

NBF Osaki Building

Kobe Port Tower

Kobe Port Tower

Beams, pipes, steel; enduring aesthetics and striking engineering spring from the same creative resource that is rejuvenating and inexhaustible.

Tokyo Station Yaesu Station Plaza (Central Ventilation Tower)

YKK 80 Building

Sophisticated environmental design is also distinguished in the **YKK 80 Building (2015)**, which presents a delicately tapestried facade onto the Akihabara area of Tokyo.

Facing westward, the entire building, serving as the headquarters of a global company, is covered in agile *sudare* screens made from extruded aluminum fragments that are thermo-regulating. This unique ensemble provides sensational perspectives both from the inside of the building and on the street level.

A vital center for exchange, reflecting and yet defying the passage of time, is the striking **Akagane Museum (2015)** in Niihama, Japan. Its three-tiered design shelters a central atrium in a circular formation, surrounded by three art galleries which together encourage an open exploration of its art spaces and small theater.

The building's brilliantly tessellated and untreated copper-plated exterior pays homage to the *akagane* (copper) mines that ensured Niihama's legendary prosperity for almost three centuries.

Asia-Pacific Import Mart (AIM)

AIM

Materializing like pointed crystal quartz in the middle of Tokyo's famed "book town", the **Jimbocho Theater Building (2007)** is a distinguished gem positioned on a small plot of precious land surrounded by narrow streets.

Its light, polyhedral steel frame and column-free spaces support an interesting steel-plated armor-like facade which functions as both a heat expansion and rainwater-channeling device. The improvised use of raw materials cleverly articulates the thespian character of this triangular building and revitalizes Jimbocho's pre-war glory days as the capital's historical performance arts hub.

Previous Pages:
Akagane Museum

Jimbocho Theater Building

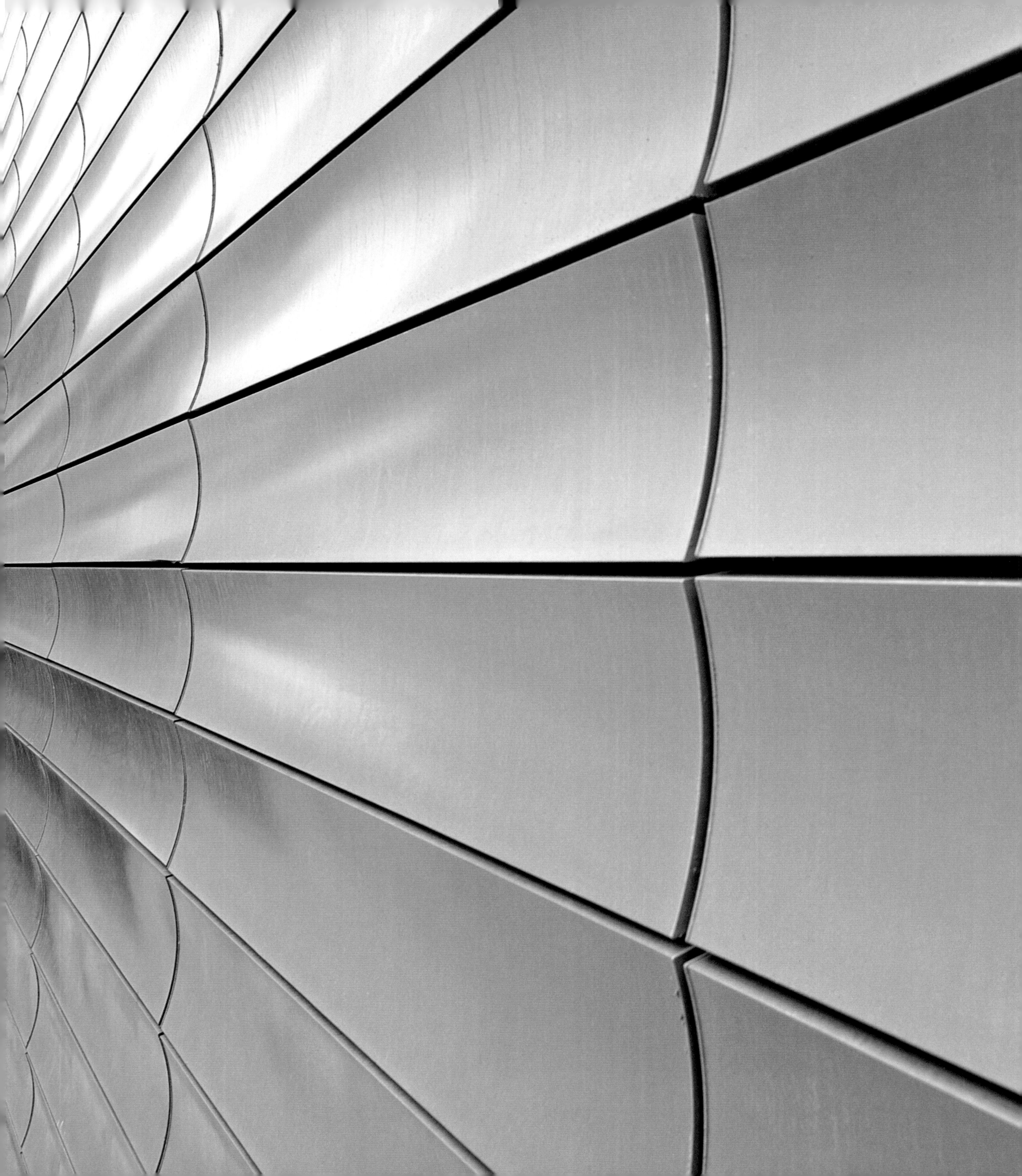

Ningbo Global Shipping Plaza

SPACES

Space might be defined as that immaterial essence which painters convey, sculptors fill, and architects envelop. Yet our relationships with architectural spaces are complex and often unconscious or elusive. Positive responses to certain objects, cultural references, and even landmarks help us to feel comfortable in or connected to certain places.

Nikken Sekkei's tireless pursuit in creating high quality spatial experiences and settings has led to the development of an entire specialized sector of their Group's practice. From refined interiors and private gardens to large community hubs and urban landscapes, one of their long-standing goals has been to develop the cause of social-environmental design, thereby cultivating the "power of space"; not only in terms of its aesthetic and technical qualities but also its capacity to enrich perception and articulate feelings and memories.

Creative, comfortable, and efficient workspaces in a minimalist style are an ever-evolving priority in highly urbanized contexts. Set within the Yodogawa Plant in Osaka, the **Daikin Technology and Innovation Center (2015)** presents an extraordinary, creative hub for global technologies. Its flexible, open plan design provides an effective interdisciplinary platform for the exchange of ideas, with intersecting meeting spaces across two vast floors.

The meticulously clean, white and futuristic look of this entire building - from its multi-faceted wall under the main escalator shaft through to its specialized experimental area in a 10-meter anechoic chamber - inspires a variety of "intellectual spaces" for innovation.

Daikin Technology and Innovation Center

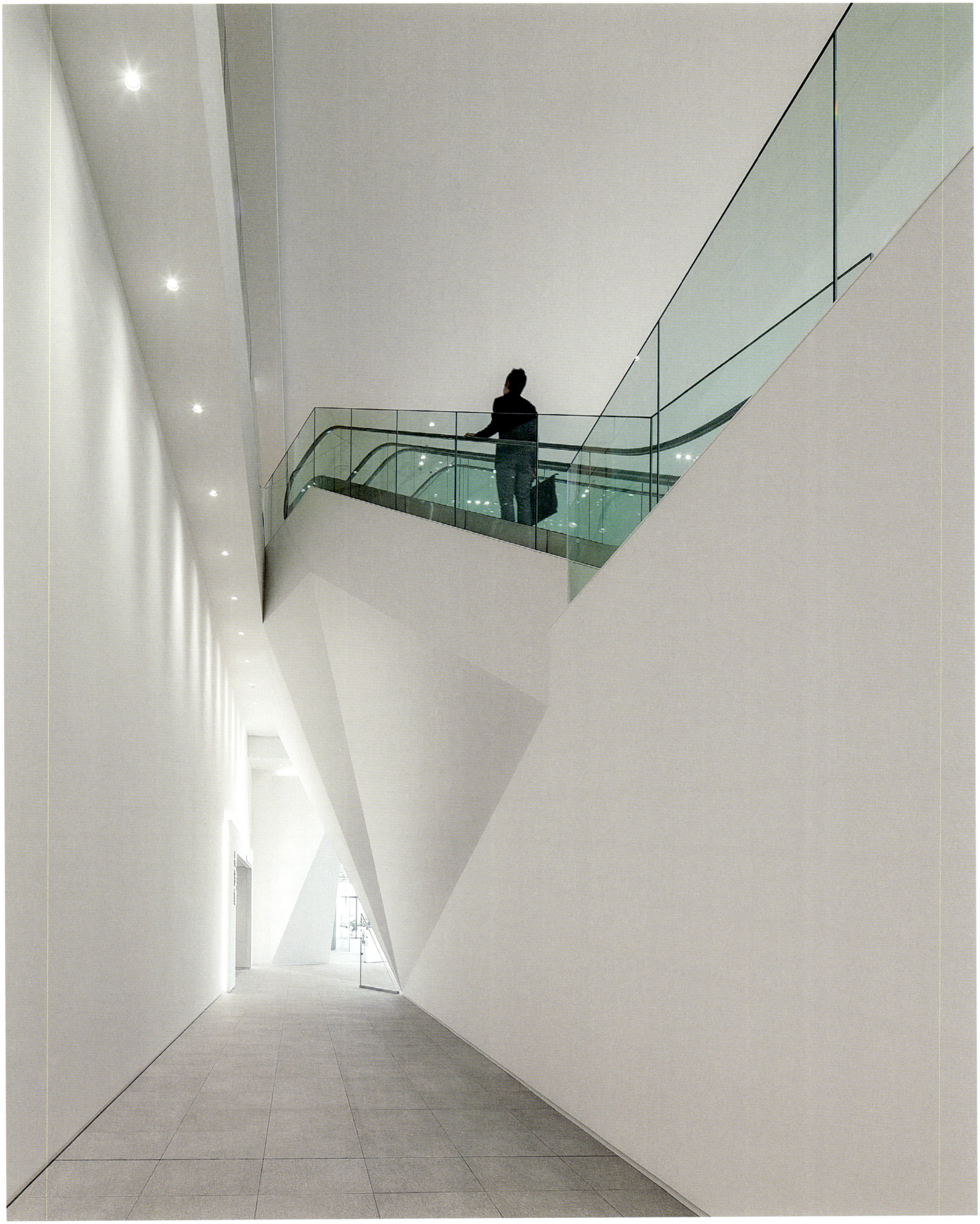

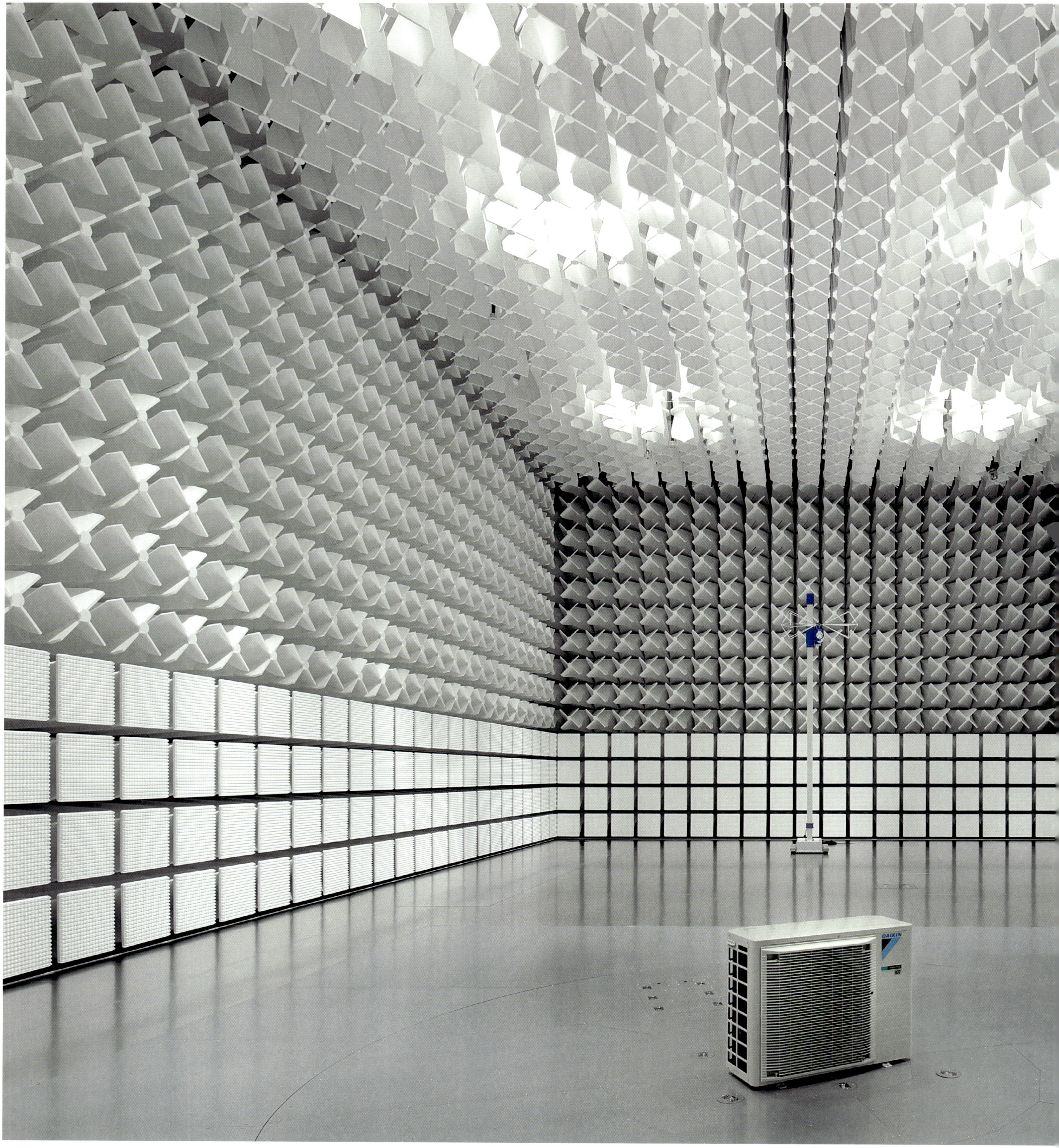
DAIKIN

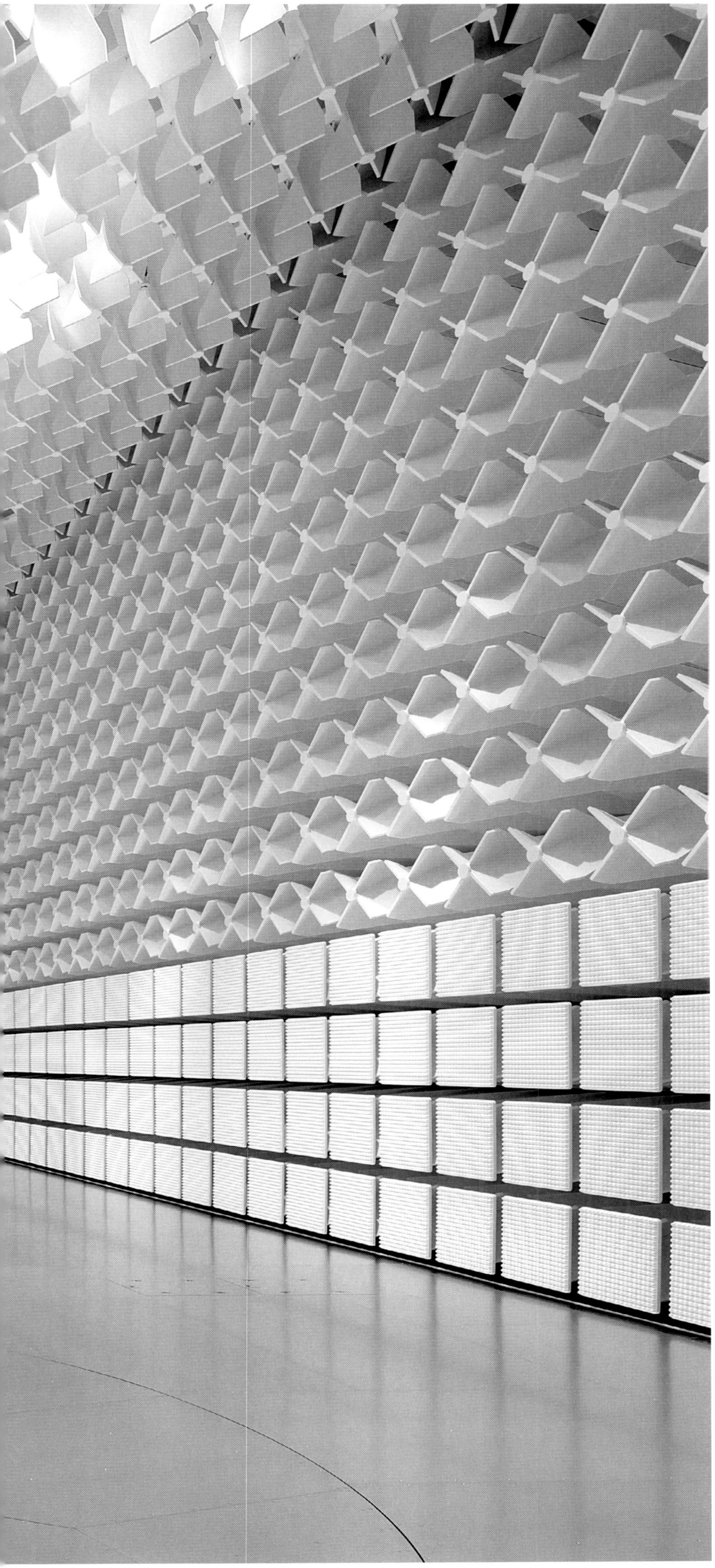

Daikin Technology and Innovation Center

Suzhou Modern Media Plaza

Super-Kamiokande, Institute for Cosmic Ray Research, The University of Tokyo

Epitomizing the ultimate influence of space both in terrestrial and celestial terms, the breathtaking scientific marvel of Japan's **Super-Kamiokande (1996)** functions as the world's largest neutrino detector. Located deep underground at Mt. Ikeno near the city of Hida in Gifu Prefecture, this state-of-the-art physics observatory observes cosmic rays and neutrinos as they pass through its central chamber, and also aims to capture traces of proton decay by detecting subatomic reactions that occur in water.

Nikken Sekkei designed the stainless-steel internal lining of its massive cylindrical tank containing ultra-pure water and other steel structures, which support many thousands of gold-hued photomultiplier tubes detecting light from Cherenkov radiation.

Many astrophysicists and other researchers from around the world have privileged access to this one-of-a-kind structure, which is simultaneously focused on inner and outer space.

Super-Kamiokande, Institute for Cosmic Ray Research, The University of Tokyo

The Museum of Oriental Ceramics, Osaka

Kyoto State Guest House

Our most cherished private spaces often balance emotional legibility with a sense of mystery, as well as visual and thought-provoking stimuli. Natural scenes are also marked by geometries and specifically alluring elements of order and variety that are like the architectural and biological "master keys" to our wellbeing.

Few buildings manage to typify these fundamental principles as graciously as the **Kyoto State Guest House (2005)**, set within Kyoto's Gyoen National Garden surrounding the city's legendary Imperial Palace. Serving as the official residence for visiting foreign dignitaries, this superbly articulated design offers an intimate and memorable retreat.

All of its interconnected rooms - arranged between *shōji* (screens) and walkways - feature subtly choreographed detailing in the highest quality Japanese crafts.

The delicate interplay of nature and human ingenuity is found here in the work of its *ningen kokuhō* (人間国宝), Japan's "living national treasures". These craftspeople are charged with preserving and passing on the country's most revered artistic traditions.

From the *sukiya* carpentry and intricate landscaping; wall length tapestries and hand-woven carpets; to its *kirikane* metallic foil motifs, Nishijin brocades and *makie* lacquers; all these elements combine to form a quintessentially peaceful backdrop throughout its unified interior and exterior spaces.

The ancient philosophy of *teioku-ichinyo* (庭屋一如), referring to the "exquisite harmony between a building and its garden", is exemplified in such dignified hospitality.

Niihama Besshi Copper Mine Memorial Library

オフィスエントランス
(タワーS) 2F
プルマン東京田町 2F
イベント広場 2F
S
P 駐車場
なぎさテラス
JR 田町駅
地下鉄 三田駅

Kobe Gakuin University Port Island Campus

Designing spaces is like composing pictures; capturing moments in still frames. After all, architecture is about creating the perfect settings for our stories.

Kyobashi Edogrand

BS-D4-3
AS-D4-4
AS-D4-3

Yamato Group Haneda Chronogate

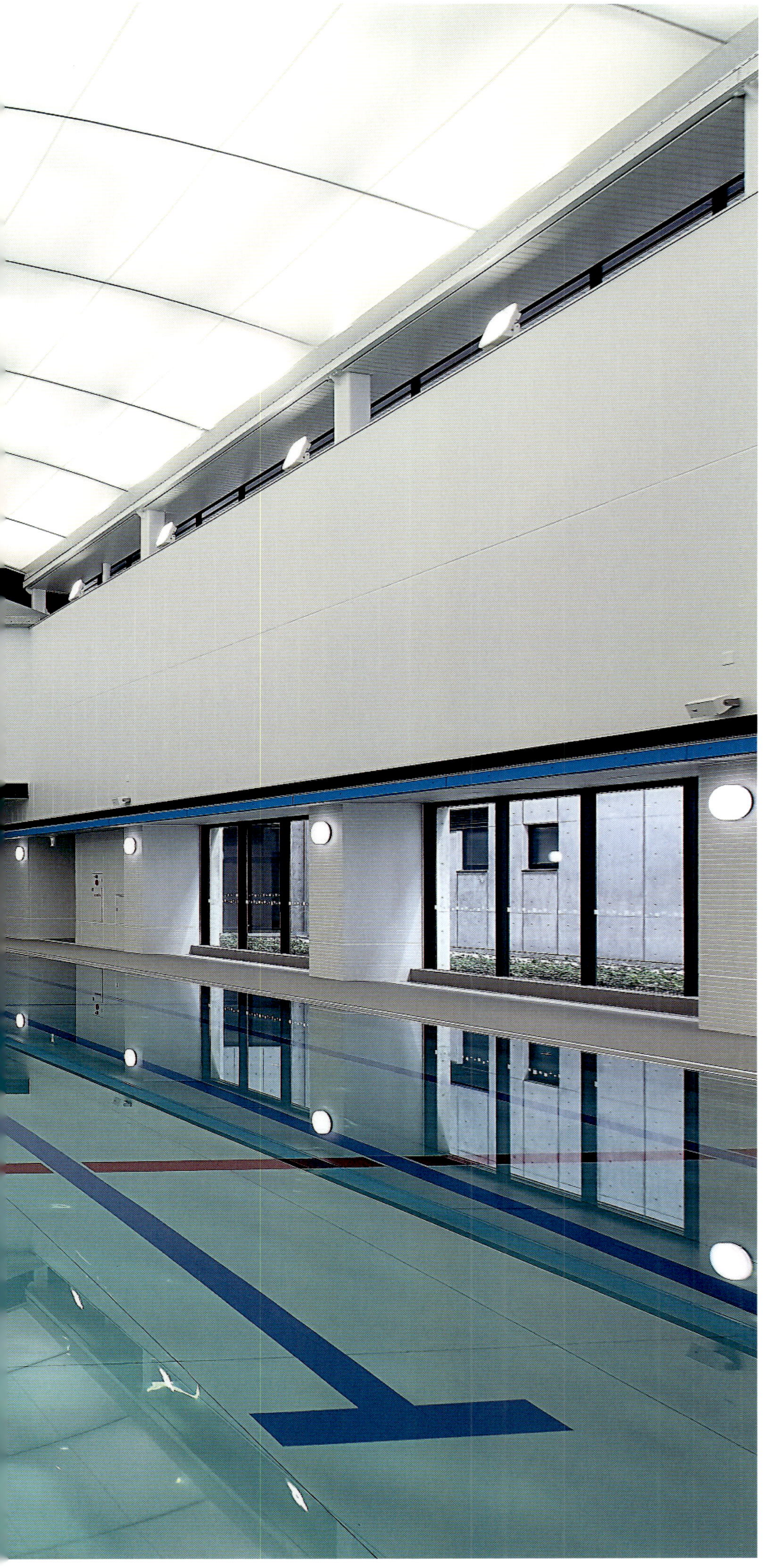

Large community spaces must cater to an endless variety of needs and expectations. People's sense of their own movement and viewing potentials are also fundamental to their positive experiences and continued feelings of belonging in these places.

Sports and entertainment venues regularly harness the collective energy of entire cross-sections of the population through generations of enthusiasts. Japan's first all weather stadium is still its largest air-supported structure. Nikken Sekkei's groundbreaking design for the **Tokyo Dome (1988)** has clearly withstood the test of time accommodating up to 55,000 people; hosting monumental events and gratifying vast audiences under a translucent glass fiber roof that quickly became an archetypal community space.

Nikken Sekkei's design for Tokyo's **Meiji Jingu Gaien Educational Training Institute (2010)**, set within the Meiji Shrine Outer Garden, even aimed to create a "small school in the forest". This remarkably calm place explores the possibilities afforded by material contrasts to achieve pleasing visual and psychological landscapes. Its sophisticated masonry network, using sheer concrete blocks arranged into open atelier style spaces, beautifully complements the native trees and environmental conditions.

Opportunities for exclusivity within public spaces are key focal points for designers of luxury hospitality.

The Ritz-Carlton, Kyoto (2013) sits along the Kamogawa River, where Kyoto's Heian noble classes (794-1185) famously positioned their legendary second residences to view the moon, overlooking the Higashiyama mountains. Inspired by the notion of accumulative "beauty with age", this building slips quietly into its abiding ambience as if it had been installed there for centuries.

Its sensual interiors communicate Japan's reverence for purity, simplicity, and forward-looking sophistication. Embracing its exterior spaces, intricate lighting details, ceiling features and ornamental placements orchestrate a refined and seductive environment on an intimate scale.

Tokyo Dome

Panasonic
MINOLTA
LaserDisc
コニカカラー
日本航空
フジカラー
日本火災
FUJI XEROX
TOYOTA

相撲
求道
木瀬部屋姫路後援会

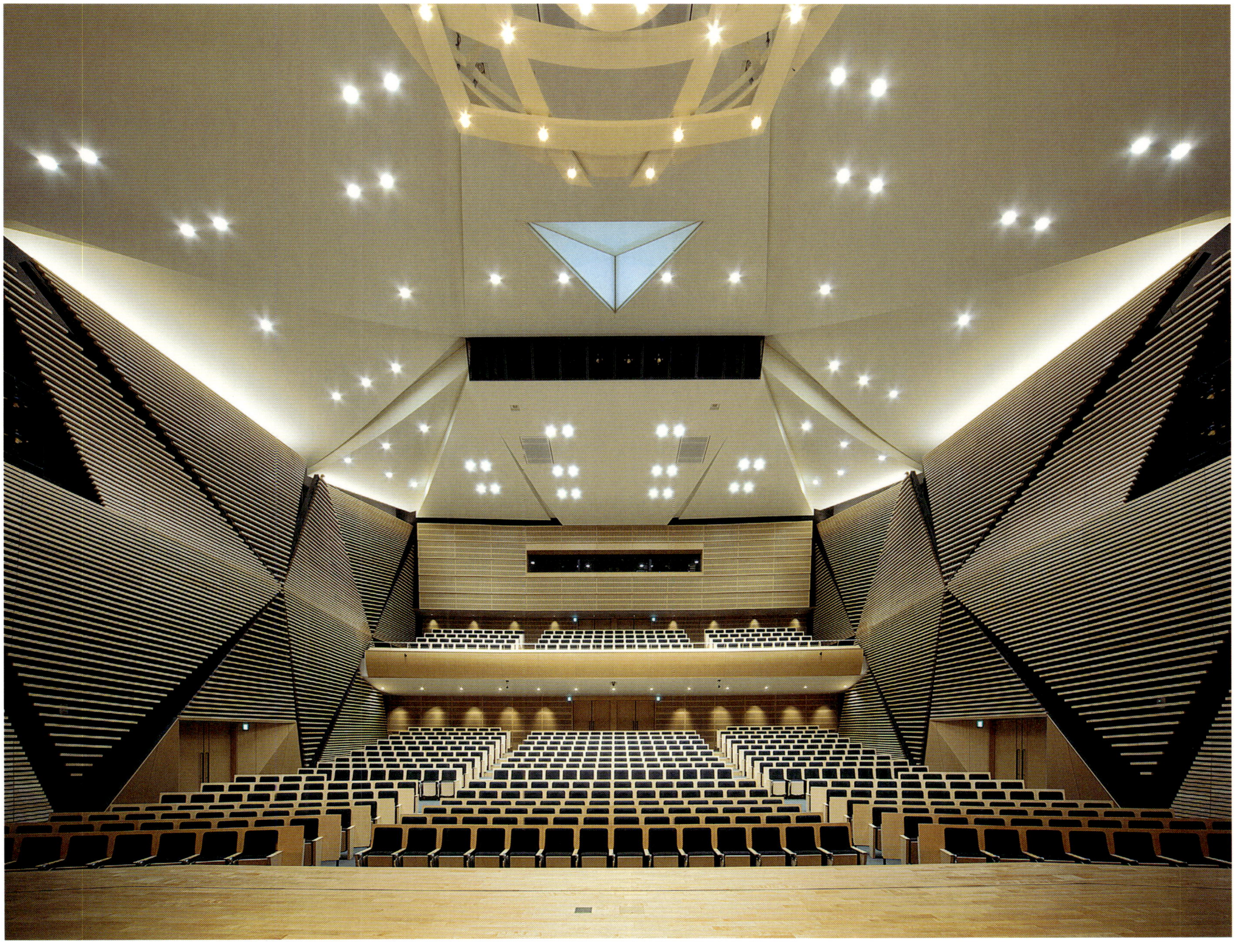

Tokyo University of Science (Katsushika Campus)

Spaces are never empty.
They have the power to draw life in.
Sometimes in human form,
other times by inviting nature,
or simply through a ray of light.

Tokyo Metropolitan Industrial Technology Research Institute

The Ritz-Carlton, Kyoto

MIDLAND SQUARE

Midland Square

Palaceside Building

Japan Cycle Sport Center

Futako Tamagawa Rise II-a

Culturally sensitive design for performance spaces and heritage buildings has been a long-standing forte of Nikken Sekkei, which also built the **Cairo National Culture Center (1988)**, situated in the capital's affluent Zamalek district. The first opera house in Egypt, it is still a key musical arts venue in the MENA region.

These majestic Arabesque geometries and clean symmetry arouse a sense of mystery and contemplation; harmonizing ancient knowledge with contemporary culture in one space and establishing a vital synergistic hub.

Cairo National Culture Center

Cairo National Culture Center

Grand Front Osaka

Kyoto Sangyo University, Sagittarius Pavilion

Shibuya Scramble Square (East Tower)

Shibuya Scramble Square (East Tower)

Buildings that quietly adorn their surroundings embody what we call contemplative architecture.

Kyoto State Guest House

Next Pages:
On the Water

ENVIRONMENTS

Growing evidence from the neurosciences across the world supports what ancient cultures and all of us as individuals have intuited since childhood: that our vitality and creativity are not only nurtured but also inextricably linked to our experiences of the natural world. The benefits of designing collaboratively alongside Mother Nature are clear and powerful tools for transforming our quality of life and urban spaces.

Japanese wisdom has reiterated its profound insights on the futility of “taming the untamable” and offered guidance on cultivating equilibrium within society and living spaces. However large or small, our homes and public buildings are part of this all-encompassing environmental continuum.

This new century is demanding our formal defense of this biological heritage. If we can truly perceive and plan for this vital union it will revolutionize our collective appreciation for the powers of good architecture to sustain and protect us.

The design for the **Okinawa Institute of Science and Technology Graduate University (2007)**, set deeply within one of the world’s great ecosystems of biodiversity - with more than 220 hectares of virgin forest surrounded by sea - exemplifies the synergy that is possible between cutting-edge science and the natural world.

Nikken Sekkei’s environmental imperatives are beautifully showcased in this extraordinary construction, which has maximized human spaces and preserved wild habitats. The building prioritizes a strong sense of interconnectedness and its contoured positioning atop mountain ridges has left the surrounding valleys intact, while minimizing the impact on the tropical forest and marine ecology.

Okinawa Institute of Science and Technology Graduate University

Boat Race Tsu

Kyoto Sangyo University, Matsunoura Seminar House

Islamic Development Bank Headquarters

Medical Rinku Port

KEYENCE

Tall and supertall buildings are the architects' responses to humanity's dream of soaring ahead.

Nikken Sekkei is actively developing more polycentric cities, designed around transportation hubs. As augmented metropolises expand skyward and underground, the "human face" of districts informs the company's longer-term plans and global strategy.

Urban environments that draw dynamic crowds become a kind of public theater. Their cross-cultural exchanges and multi-functional qualities like in nature - from its basic chromosomal origins to its expansive eco-systems - inspire the conceptual thinking behind these new "urban habitats".

One of the largest port cities in Japan, Kobe has been an important trading center since the country reopened after more than 200 years, and its "harborland" skyline boasts a unique combination of cultural influences. The **Kobe Port Tower (1963)**, Kobe Maritime Museum (1987), and Kobe Kanden Building (1999), all designed by Nikken Sekkei, are architectural manifestations of how this waterfront has been shaped by its vital relationships to the sea.

Based on the idea of the transport hub as a self-sustaining community, the **Tokyo Station Yaesu Development (2013)** culminated in the "Tokyo Station City" landmark. Under a vast "GranRoof" resembling the sails of a majestic ship, this design forms a gateway between the historic Marunouchi-side of the station building - restored to its original 1914 state - and the Yaesu-side of Tokyo Station, as the new face of the capital expressing advanced urban technologies. Its beautiful pedestrian landscape includes native vegetation across the four seasons; interlacing nature's grounding qualities with the skyward spirit of its crystal-like buildings.

Shibuya Scramble Square (East Tower)

Next Pages:
Queen's Square Yokohama

Queen's Tower A

19:10

BE·PORT OF K

Looking ahead,
cities will be there,
buildings will be there,
even for hundreds of years.
And we will live within
and alongside them,
as memories of the past
and inspirations for
the future.

Previous Pages:
Kobe Port

Sumitomo Life Insurance Company Midosuji Building
(Currently known as Resorttrust, Inc. Midosuji Building)

World Trade Center Seoul

Tokyo Station Yaesu Development - GranRoof

JR 東京駅
Tokyo Station

コスモ証券

Nippon Life Insurance Company Head Office

日本生命

Palaceside Building

リーダース ダイジェスト

Waseda University Senior High School, Auditorium

Kyoto State Guest House

OSAKA-JO HALL
大阪城ホー

Osaka-Jo Hall

The concept of buildings being "territorial entities" is showcased in the company's magnificent design for the **Pola Museum of Art (2002)**, which makes enviable use of the lush topography in Japan's Kanagawa Prefecture. Embedded within the Sengokuhara region, it stretches across the native vegetation while most of its spaces are nestled below ground level. With minimal disturbance to the national park, its regenerative effects extend into art and nature trails through this biodiversity.

Whether as a giant lying on the forest floor or a spaceship landed on Earth, this remarkable building represents a corporeal desire to restore our relationship with nature; and perhaps even following the Japanese philosophy of *shinrin-yoku* (forest bathing).

An extremely ambitious and innovative mega-project is currently underway in Japan which will surely manifest the best of both worlds, and create unprecedented interfaces for sustainability and innovation between people and their urban environments.

The world's tallest timber tower, planned for Tokyo within its **W350 Plan (2041)**, is a technology-based research development project that is exploring future possibilities, using the tangible and symbolic significance of wood and its natural affinities with human beings.

The Sumitomo Forestry Company and Nikken Sekkei have partnered to create a 70-story hybrid multi-use building consisting of 90% timber, with spacious balconies covered in native vegetation; elevating the entire concept of environmentally conscious and sustainable "city forests" into a new way of living.

Mitsui Sumitomo Insurance Surugadai Building and Surugadai Annex Building

Next Pages:
Cityplaza Osaka

STOP
STOP
STOP
STOP
R
275
BUS
OUT
IN
P

A society that puts itself
above the natural world
is condemned to failure.
We strive to propose
architectural and engineering
solutions that inspire,
reflect, and coexist
with the environment.

Sustainability is about
reducing our impact on Earth
but also about giving Mother
Nature new occasions to prosper.

Previous Pages:
Shanghai Greenland Center

Blurring the lines between natural design and craftsmanship has always been in Japan's DNA; it's the cultural baton we are passing on across generations for a more conscious way of living and a happier future.

Previous Pages:
Okinawa Institute of Science and Technology Graduate University

POLA Museum of Arts

It is a great pleasure to have produced this beautiful book during challenging times and I sincerely thank all those who have made it possible, across the various time zones. We hope your enjoyment of this publication, which is essentially a collective invitation towards an exciting future, matches our pride in the design legacy we have worked to maintain throughout our 120 years.

Since its foundations in 1900, Nikken Sekkei has nurtured the energy and intuitions of its new generation professionals, while at the same time respecting the experiences and insights of its forebears. As we now celebrate this important anniversary, a global effort for cleaner, renewable energy systems and meeting sustainability objectives is taking place. These new organizational conditions and imperatives present more opportunities for innovation, coordination, and collaboration, which are the hallmarks of our company.

We are working to strengthen our relationships with our partners who share our values and commitments; aiming together to plan, design, and build places where people love to work, learn, and relax, which all contributes to creating resilient and dynamic cities.

We began with twenty-six professionals over a century ago and now our Nikken Group members total over 2,800 employees. Following our philosophy of "EXPERIENCE, INTEGRATED" across our trusted network of architects, engineers, designers, planners, and clients, we are constantly focused on developing centers of excellence to produce architectures that enhance the quality of life. Some of our key contributions have been in the roles of long-term urban redevelopment; designing with nature; and building future-oriented projects which respond to the way people use and relate to spaces.

The year 2020 has presented a global dilemma that is compelling everyone across the planet to assess their own social and environmental responsibilities. Such a pivotal moment cannot be ignored. Adapting to the immutability of change is one of our core principles, and we have diligently continued this original pledge, which I call "flexible creativity".

New technological advancements and artificial intelligence are evolving remarkable scenarios that will enable the best architectural ideas to realize unprecedented achievements. Nikken Sekkei is deeply involved in groundbreaking projects related to sustainably "smarter cities", working on solutions for better ways of living. The protection of our environmental health is one of our founding values and the priority now is to invite nature back into our cities.

Our vision is to expand out from Japan, bringing our professional expertise to aesthetically distinguished and socially conscious international projects, committed to manifesting excellence in spatial envirorments. I am proud of our creative alliances in many parts of Asia, the Middle East, and more recently Europe, which together form an extraordinary tapestry of talent and ideas.

My wish for the indefinite future is a company that continues to sail through time with the same integrity, responsibility and powers of imagination that have led Nikken Sekkei to this day, with an open outlook onto tomorrow.

Tadao Kamei
CEO and President
NIKKEN SEKKEI, Japan

PROJECTS

A

Aichi University of the Arts, Music Department Building

Construction site:
Aichi, Japan
Completion year:
2013
Page:
99

Akagane Museum

Construction site:
Ehime, Japan
Completion year:
2015
Pages:
116-117

Anan City Office

Construction site:
Tokushima, Japan
Completion year:
2017
Pages:
98, 103

ARAKAWA BLDG.

Construction site:
Tokyo, Japan
Completion year:
2018
Page:
193

Asia-Pacific Import Mart (AIM)

Construction site:
Fukuoka, Japan
Completion year:
1998
Pages:
114-115

B

Beijing Media Network, BMN

Construction site:
Beijing, China
Completion year:
2008
Page:
126

Boat Race Tsu

Construction site:
Mie, Japan
Completion year:
2002
Pages:
178, 180

C

Cairo National Culture Center

Construction site:
Cairo, Egypt
Completion year:
1988
Pages:
164, 165

CITIC Plaza

Construction site:
Shanghai, China
Completion year:
2011
Page:
72

Cityplaza Osaka

Construction site:
Osaka, Japan
Completion year:
2006
Pages:
216-217

Conrad Osaka

Construction site:
Osaka, Japan
Completion year:
2017
Page:
60

D

Daido Life Insurance Company Osaka Head Office Building

Construction site:
Osaka City, Japan
Completion year:
1993
Page:
91

Daiichi Sankyo Shinagawa R & D Center

Construction site:
Tokyo, Japan
Completion year:
2016
Pages:
86-87

Daikin Technology and Innovation Center

Construction site:
Osaka, Japan
Completion year:
2015
Pages:
123, 124

F

Futako Tamagawa Rise II-a

Construction site:
Tokyo, Japan
Completion year:
2015
Page:
161

G

Gas Science Museum

Construction site:
Tokyo, Japan
Completion year:
2006
Page:
209

Grand Front Osaka

Construction site:
Osaka City, Japan
Completion year:
2013
Page:
166

Guangzhou Library

Construction site:
Guangzhou, China
Completion year:
2012
Pages:
36, 90

H

Hoki Museum

Construction site:
Chiba, Japan
Completion year:
2010
Page:
53

I

IBM Japan Headquarters

Construction site:
Tokyo, Japan
Completion year:
1971
Page:
50

Islamic Development Bank Headquarters

Construction site:
Jeddah, Kingdom of Saudi Arabia
Completion year:
1993
Pages:
31, 182

J

Japan Cycle Sport Center

Construction site:
Shizuoka, Japan
Completion year:
1971
Page:
159

Japan Pavilion Expo 70

Construction site:
Osaka, Japan
Completion year:
1970
Page:
27

Jimbocho Theater Building

Construction site:
Tokyo, Japan
Completion year:
2007
Page:
118

JRC Advanced Technology Center

Construction site:
Nagano, Japan
Completion year:
2014
Pages:
42, 43

K

Kakegawa City Hall

Construction site:
Shizuoka, Japan
Completion year:
1996
Page:
19

Kawai-cho Comprehensive Welfare Center

Construction site:
Nara, Japan
Completion year:
2000
Page:
153

Keihanna Plaza

Construction site:
Kyoto, Japan
Completion year:
1993
Page:
62

Keyence Corporation Head Office and Laboratory

Construction site:
Osaka City, Japan
Completion year:
1994
Page:
184

Kise Sumo Stable

Construction site:
Tokyo, Japan
Completion year:
2006
Page:
150

Kobe Gakuin University Port Island Campus

Construction site:
Hyogo, Japan
Completion year:
2007
Page:
140

Kobe International House

Construction site:
Hyogo, Japan
Completion year:
1999
Page:
26

Kobe Port Tower

Construction site:
Hyogo, Japan
Completion year:
1963
Pages:
106, 107, 190-191

Kyobashi Edogrand

Construction site:
Tokyo, Japan
Completion year:
2016
Page:
143

Kyoto Sangyo University, Matsunoura Seminar House

Construction site:
Shiga, Japan
Completion year:
2001
Page:
181

Kyoto Sangyo University, Sagittarius Pavilion

Construction site:
Kyoto, Japan
Completion year:
2016
Page:
167

Kyoto State Guest House

Construction site:
Kyoto, Japan
Completion year:
2006
Pages:
133, 134, 171, 211

M

Mainichi Broadcasting Headquarters Building

Construction site:
Osaka, Japan
Completion year:
1990
Page:
68

Marukyu Building

Construction site:
Saitama, Japan
Completion year:
2000
Page:
58

Medical Rinku Port

Construction site:
Osaka, Japan
Completion year:
2016
Page:
183

Meiji Innovation Center

Construction site:
Tokyo, Japan
Completion year:
2017
Page:
111

Meiji Jingu Gaien Educational Training Institute

Construction site:
Tokyo, Japan
Completion year:
2010
Pages:
162, 163

Menara Astra

Construction site:
Jakarta, Indonesia
Completion year:
2017
Page:
34

Midland Square

Construction site:
Aichi, Japan
Completion year:
2006
Pages:
45, 156

Mitsui Sumitomo Insurance Surugadai Building and Surugadai Annex Building

Construction site:
Tokyo, Japan
Completion year:
2013
Pages:
24-25, 215

Mode Gakuen Spiral Towers

Construction site:
Nagoya, Japan
Completion year:
2008
Page:
37

Mokuzai Kaikan

Construction site:
Tokyo, Japan
Completion year:
2009
Pages:
100, 101

msb Tamachi Station Tower N

Construction site:
Tokyo, Japan
Completion year:
2020
Page:
139

N

Nakamura Gakuen Girl's Junior and Senior High School

Construction site:
Fukuoka, Japan
Completion year:
2010
Page:
138

Nakanoshima Festival Tower

Construction site:
Osaka, Japan
Completion year:
2012
Pages:
64, 65

NBF Osaki Building

Construction site:
Tokyo, Japan
Completion year:
2011
Pages:
92, 104, 110

NEC Head Office (NEC Super Tower)

Construction site:
Tokyo, Japan
Completion year:
1990
Page:
49

Niihama Besshi Copper Mine Memorial Library

Construction site:
Ehime, Japan
Completion year:
1998
Page:
136

Nikkei Head Office

Construction site:
Tokyo, Japan
Completion year:
2009
Page:
67

Ningbo Global Shipping Plaza

Construction site:
Zheijang, China
Completion year:
2015
Page:
120

Nippon Life Insurance Company Head Office

Construction site:
Osaka, Japan
Completion year:
1939, 1962, 2015
Page:
203

Nippon Life Insurance Marunouchi Building

Construction site:
Tokyo, Japan
Completion year:
2004
Page:
95

O

Okabe Headquarters Building

Construction site:
Tokyo, Japan
Completion year:
2013
Page:
75

Okata Port Passenger Shelter / Tsunami Evacuation Facility

Construction site:
Tokyo, Japan
Completion year:
2019
Page:
56

P

Q

R

Resorttrust, Inc. Midosuji Building

Construction site:
Osaka, Japan
Completion year:
1983
Page:
194

S

Saitama Super Arena

Construction site:
Saitama, Japan
Completion year:
2000
Page:
78

San-Ai Dream Center

Construction site:
Tokyo, Japan
Completion year:
1963
Pages:
32, 33

Sendai International Airport

Construction site:
Miyagi, Japan
Completion year:
1997
Page:
63

Shanghai Greenland Center

Construction site:
Shanghai, China
Completion year:
2017
Pages:
218-219

Shibuya Scramble Square (East Tower)

Construction site:
Tokyo, Japan
Completion year:
2019
Pages:
168, 169, 187

Shinjuku NS Building

Construction site:
Tokyo, Japan
Completion year:
1982
Page:
74

Shinjuku Sumitomo Building

Construction site:
Tokyo, Japan
Completion year:
1974 and 2020
Pages:
39, 51

St Luke's International Hospital

Construction site:
Tokyo, Japan
Completion year:
1992
Page:
46

Sumitomo Building

Construction site:
Osaka, Japan
Completion year:
1930
Page:
199

Sumitomo Fudosan Azabu-Juban Building

Construction site:
Tokyo, Japan
Completion year:
2017
Pages:
Cover, 71

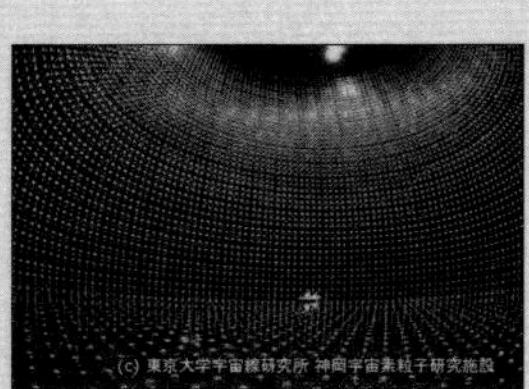

Super-Kamiokande, Institute for Cosmic Ray Research, The University of Tokyo

Construction site:
Gifu, Japan
Completion year:
1995
Pages:
128, 130, 131

Suzhou Modern Media Plaza

Construction site:
Suzhou, China
Completion year:
2016
Pages:
73, 127

T

The Museum of Oriental Ceramics, Osaka

Construction site:
Osaka, Japan
Completion year:
1982 and 1998
Page:
132

The Ritz-Carlton, Kyoto

Construction site:
Kyoto, Japan
Completion year:
2013
Page:
155

The Yomiuri Shimbun Building

Construction site:
Tokyo, Japan
Completion year:
2013
Page:
96

Toho Gakuen School of Music

Construction site:
Tokyo, Japan
Completion year:
2014
Pages:
55, 97

Tokyo Dome

Construction site:
Tokyo, Japan
Completion year:
1988
Page:
149

Tokyo Metropolitan Industrial Technology Research Institute

Construction site:
Tokyo, Japan
Completion year:
2011
Page:
154

Tokyo Midtown

Construction site:
Tokyo, Japan
Completion year:
2007
Page:
77

Tokyu Plaza Ginza

Construction site:
Tokyo, Japan
Completion year:
2016
Pages:
14, 80-81

TOKYO SKYTREE

Construction site:
Tokyo, Japan
Completion year:
2012
Page:
4

Tokyo Station Yaesu Development (GranRoof)

Tokyo Station Yaesu Station Plaza

Construction site:
Tokyo, Japan
Completion year:
2013 (GranRoof),
2014 (Station Plaza)
Pages:
196-197 (GranRoof)
109 (Station Plaza)

Tokyo Tower

Construction site:
Tokyo, Japan
Completion year:
1958
Pages:
16-17

Tokyo University of Science (Katsushika Campus)

Construction site:
Tokyo, Japan
Completion year:
2013
Page:
151

Toslove Hakone Viole

Construction site:
Kanagawa, Japan
Completion year:
2000
Page:
27

Tsu City Business and Sports Center

Construction site:
Mie, Japan
Completion year:
2017
Page:
146

Tsurumi University

Construction site:
Kanagawa, Japan
Completion year:
1997
Page:
21

W

Waseda University Senior High School, Auditorium

Construction site:
Tokyo, Japan
Completion year:
2014
Pages:
89, 206-207

World Trade Center Seoul

Construction site:
Seoul, Korea
Completion year:
1988
Page:
195

Y

Yamato Group Haneda Chronogate

Construction site:
Tokyo, Japan
Completion year:
2013
Pages:
23, 144

YKK 80 Building

Construction site:
Tokyo, Japan
Completion year:
2015
Page:
112

Yokohama Mitsui Building

Construction site:
Kanagawa, Japan
Completion year:
2012
Page:
84

Special thanks:

Nikken Sekkei would like to express its sincere appreciation and highest esteem for the numerous clients and professionals who have entrusted their projects and collaborated with the company over its 120 years.

Our profound gratitude also goes to Mrs Shoei Nakawake for her *Shodo* calligraphy and precious support in the making of this book.

NIKKEN SEKKEI LTD acknowledges:

Management and supervision:
Hiroaki Otani, Fadi Jabri, Kenji Senoo, Tetsuto Furuhata

Creative direction and copywriting:
Raffaella Bedini

Creative support and administration:
Kumiko Fukuyama

Creative assistance:
Kazuki Makimura, Masaya Aoki

Image research and coordination:
Taro Chiba, Takako Saigou, Mamoru Maeda, Akiko Arakawa

Image credits:

CENTER PHOTO JAPAN: p. 146
Daici Ano: p. 206
FOTOTECA, Katsuhisa Kida: p. 63
Fuminari Yamamoto: p. 184
Getty Images: pp. 4, 16-17 (©2015 Bohistock), 33 (©Bettmann Archive), 107, 231 (©Bernardo Ricci Armani), 130 (©2015 The Asahi Shimbun), 188-189, 190-191(©kwanchai_k).
Harunori Noda [Gankohsha]: pp. 23, 24-25, 53, 55, 75, 92, 96, 97, 104, 110, 118, 145, 172-173, 193, 215
Higashide Photo Studio: pp. 64, 65, 98, 103, 167
Hiroyuki Hirai: pp. 162, 163
Hu Wenkit: pp. 36, 73, 90, 120
Kamioka Observatory, ICRR (Institute for Cosmic Ray Research), The University of Tokyo: pp. 128, 131
Kaneaki Monma: pp. 49, 50
Katsuaki Furudate: pp. 164; 165
Katsuta Shouya: p. 77
Kawasumi•Kobayashi Kenji Photograph Office: pp. 39, 51
Kazuo Natori [Studio Natori]: p. 106
Ken'ichi Suzuki: p. 112
Kiyohiko Higashide: pp. 40, 62, 68, 83, 114-115, 195
Koji Horiuchi: pp. 45, 67, 84, 156, 209
Koji Yamazaki [Prise]: p. 183
KOKYU MIWA ARCHITECTURAL PHOTOGRAPHY: pp. 78, 136, 151, 203, 222-223
Kouji Okamoto [Techni Staff]: pp. 26, 38
Kouzan Shimizu: p. 123
LIXIL Corporation: p. 91
Mamoru Ishiguro: p. 224
Masafumi Koda: p. 153
Masao Arai: p. 20
Minoru Iwasaki: p. 126
Minoru Karamatsu: p. 194
mintwow: pp. 218-219
Nakasa & Partners: pp. 14, 27, 60, 72, 80-81, 100, 101, 116-117, 155, 174
NARU Architectural Photography Office: p. 34
NIKKEN SEKKEI LTD Archive: pp. 27, 56, 166, 199, 200
NIKKEN SEKKEI LTD Drawing Department: p. 32
Nisinihon Shaboh Fukuoka: p. 138
Osamu Murai: pp. 22, 37, 74, 95, 171, 204
Qin Wei: p. 127
Rainer Viertlböck: pp. 196-197
Richard Bryant: pp. 31, 182
Satoru Mishima: p. 21
Satoshi Asakawa: p. 177
Seigan Kuroda: p. 28
Shibuya Scramble Square: pp. 168, 169
Shinkenchiku-sha: pp. 159, 211
Shinozawa Architectural Photograph Office: pp. 42, 43, 133, 134, 150
SHINWA: pp. 132; 216-217
SHIYO KAWAI: pp. 140, 212
SS Co., Ltd.: pp. 19, 46, 58, 71, 86-87, 89, 99, 109, 111, 124, 139, 154, 161, 178, 180, 181, 187, and cover
SS KIKAKU: p. 143
Syuji Yamada: pp. 137, 158
Watanabe Studio: p. 149

Photo credits (pp. 228-237):

CENTER PHOTO JAPAN: Tsu City Business and Sports Center
Fernando GomuLya: Menara Astra
FOTOTECA, Katsuhisa Kida: Sendai International Airport
Getty Images: Kobe Port Tower (©Bernardo Ricci Armani)
Harunori Noda [Gankohsha]: ARAKAWA BLDG.; Hoki Museum; Jimbocho Theater Building; Mitsui Sumitomo Insurance Surugadai Building and Surugadai Annex Building; Mokuzai Kaikan; NBF Osaki Building; Okabe Headquarters Building; On the Water; Toho Gakuen School of Music
Higashide Photo Studio: Akagane Museum; Anan City Office
Hiroyuki Hirai: Meiji Jingu Gaien Educational Training Institute
Hu Wenkit: Ningbo Global Shipping Plaza; Guangzhou Library; Suzhou Modern Media Plaza
Kamioka Observatory, ICRR (Institute for Cosmic Ray Research), The University of Tokyo: Super-Kamiokande, Institute for Cosmic Ray Research, The University of Tokyo
Kaneaki Monma: IBM Japan Headquarters; NEC Head Office (NEC Super Tower)
Karoku Kato: Mainichi Broadcasting Headquarters Building
Katsuaki Furudate: Cairo National Culture Center
Kawasumi•Kobayashi Kenji Photograph Office: San-ai Dream Center; Tokyo Midtown
Kazuo Natori [Studio Natori]: Cityplaza Osaka
Ken'ichi Suzuki: Gas Science Museum
Kiyohiko Higashide: Keihanna Plaza; Osaka Bar Association Building; World Trade Center Seoul
Koji Horiuchi: Midland Square; Nikkei Head Office; Yokohama Mitsui Building
Koji Yamazaki [Prise]: Medical Rinku Port, The Ritz-Carlton, Kyoto
KOKYU MIWA ARCHITECTURAL PHOTOGRAPHY: Saitama Super Arena
Kouji Okamoto [Techni Staff]: Kobe International House; Nippon Life Insurance Company Head Office; Okinawa Institute of Science and Technology Graduate University; Tokyo University of Science (Katsushika Campus)
Kouzan Shimizu: Daikin Technology and Innovation Center
Mamoru Ishiguro: POLA Museum of Arts
Masafumi Koda: Kawai-cho Comprehensive Welfare Center
Minoru Iwasaki: Beijing Media Network, BMN
Minoru Karamatsu: Keyence Corporation Head Office and Laboratory; Osaka Prefectural Nakanoshima Library; Resorttrust, Inc. Midosuji Building
mintwow: Shanghai Greenland Center
Nakasa & Partners: CITIC Plaza; Conrad Osaka; Toslove Hakone Viole
NIKKEN SEKKEI LTD ARCHIVE: Grand Front Osaka; Japan Pavilion Expo 70; Sumitomo Building; Osaka Securities Exchange Building; Okata Port Passenger Shelter / Tsunami Evacuation Facility; Shinjuku NS Building
Nisinihon Shaboh Fukuoka: Nakamura Gakuen Girl's Junior and Senior High School
Osamu Murai: Mode Gakuen Spiral Towers; Niihama Besshi Copper Mine Memorial Library; Nippon Life Insurance Marunouchi Building; Palaceside Building
Photo Communication Inc.: Kyoto Sangyo University, Sagittarius Pavilion
Rainer Viertlböck: Tokyo Station Yaesu Development (GranRoof); Tokyo Station Yaesu Station Plaza; YKK 80 Building
Richard Bryant: Islamic Development Bank Headquarters
Ryota Atarashi: TOKYO SKYTREE
Satoru Mishima: Tsurumi University
Seigan Kuroda: Daido Life Insurance Company, Osaka Head Office Building; Osaka City Air Terminal (OCAT)
Shinkenchiku-sha: Kyoto State Guest House; Osaka World Trade Center Building (Cosmo Tower); Yamato Group Haneda Chronogate
Shinozawa Architectural Photograph Office: JRC Advanced Technology Center; Kise Sumo Stable; Meiji Innovation Center; Tokyo Tower
SHINWA: The Museum of Oriental Ceramics, Osaka
SHIYO KAWAI: Kobe Gakuin University Port Island Campus; Osaka-Jo Hall
SS Co., Ltd: Aichi University of the Arts, Music Department Building; Asia-Pacific Import Mart (AIM); Boat Race Tsu; Daiichi Sankyo Shinagawa R & D Center; Futako Tamagawa Rise II-a; Kakegawa City Hall; Kyobashi Edogrand; Kyoto Sangyo University, Matsunoura Seminar House; Marukyu Building; msb Tamachi Station Tower N; Shibuya Scramble Square (East Tower); Shinjuku Sumitomo Building; St Luke's International Hospital; Sumitomo Fudosan Azabu-Juban Building; The Yomiuri Shimbun Building; Tokyo Metropolitan Industrial Technology Research Institute; Tokyu Plaza Ginza; Waseda University Senior High School, Auditorium
Taisuke Ogawa: Japan Cycle Sport Center; Queen's Square Yokohama
TAKENAKA CORPORATION: Nakanoshima Festival Tower
Watanabe Studio: Tokyo Dome

Editor
Rosa Maria Falvo

Design
Giulio Cubo Ferrarella

Images courtesy of NIKKEN SEKKEI LTD

Texts by
Rosa Maria Falvo

Distributed in English throughout the world by
Rizzoli International Publications Inc.
300 Park Avenue South,
New York, NY 10010, USA

ISBN: 978-8-8918-2996-2
2021 2022 2023 2024 / 10 9 8 7 6 5 4 3 2 1

First edition March 2021

This volume was printed by Editoriale Bortolazzi Stei S.r.l.,

Printed in Italy